CREATIVE IDEAS
FOR
THANKSGIVING

edited by Linda S. Davidson

CREATIVE IDEAS FOR THANKSGIVING
Edited by Linda S. Davidson

ISBN 0-940754-75-4

EDUCATIONAL MINISTRIES, INC.

TABLE OF CONTENTS

INTRODUCTION

This book is presented as a resource for creative planning of Thanksgiving activities in the church. The material is divided into three sections: Worship; Stories, Poems and Plays; and Activities. This does not mean that material found in one section should be limited to that area of programming. We are offering a large variety of material for you to pick and choose from according to your particular needs. For instance, if you plan a Family Thanksgiving Festival at your church the Sunday before Thanksgiving, you will certainly select material from all three sections of the book. We hope that you will find material here to help your congregation appreciate their many blessings and offer their thanks and praise to our Father.

WORSHIP

GIVING THANKS JOYFULLY

by Judy Gattis Smith

Order of Service

Joyfully Gathering to Worship
    Opening Remarks
    Psalm 100 — Fanfare & Procession of Children
    Hymn: "Joyful, Joyful We Adore Thee"
    Statement of Theme
    Song: "Hallelujah"
Joyfully Affirming Our Faith
    Responsive Reading
    Litany with Clapping Refrain
Recalling Our Blessings
    Meditation with Colors
    Hymn: "All Things Bright and Beautiful"
Expressing Our Thanks

Work of the Planning Committee

1. Go over the suggested program together, deciding on changes that will best fit your group.

2. Arrange for someone to play trumpet fanfare.

3. Choose child or youth to read the Reader's part in the Responsive Reading.

4. Practice the three songs: "Joyful, Joyful We Adore Thee," "Hallelujah," and "All Things Bright and Beautiful," or choose other hymns or songs which you prefer, or write your own.

5. Practice clapping response to the Litany, Psalm 136. You may need someone with musical experience to help you.

6. Make or purchase large sheets of poster board in yellow, green, red, orange, white, and blue. Decide which children will carry these.

7. If it is appropriate to decorate your setting for the service have the committee make montages fol-lowing the colors of thanksgiving theme. Cut pictures from magazines of things for which we are thankful. Color coordinate these. Arrange the pictures in any order. Have an all yellow montage, etc.

The purpose of this liturgy is to capture the joyfulness and exuberance of children and channel it into a service of thanksgiving to God.

Giving Thanks Joyfully

Leader: Good morning and welcome to our children's liturgy of thanks. For some reason, we seem to think of worship as a quiet time, a still moment. In worship services our tone of voice tends to be hushed and solemn. We tiptoe about or shuffle slowly and silently. Yet, if we read honestly many of the Bible stories or accounts of early worship we find these experiences vibrating with noise. In describing the anointing of Solomon as king of Israel, for example, the Bible reads, "trumpets blare, all the people shouted, 'Long live King Solomon,' and they escorted him home in procession with great rejoicing and playing of pipes so that *the very earth split with noise."* (1 Kings 1:39,40)

We come here today to give thanks. May we enter into this service with great rejoicing and exuberant sound.

Voice: *(From back of room)* "Make a joyful noise unto the Lord, all ye lands!" *(Trumpet plays fanfare)*

"Serve the Lord with gladness, come before his presence with singing." *(Children enter singing, "Joyful, Joyful We Adore Thee"—they may skip in—congregation joins in the singing.)*

"Know ye that the Lord he is God. It is he that hath made us and not we ourselves. We are his people and the sheep of his pasture. Enter his gates with thanksgiving and his courts with praise. Be thankful unto him and bless his name. For the Lord is good. His mercy is everlasting and his truth endureth to all generations."

Leader: We gather today to thank God for goodness and for everlasting mercy. An ancient creed of the church says, "We do kneel with thousands of cherubims singing Alleluia and many times 10,000 seraphims and archangels acclaiming thine holiness, worshiping, confessing and praising Thee." We join our voices with the multitudes who sing thy praises and proclaim thy wonders and majesty. We now become a part of the whole spiritual universe which exists to declare the glory of God.

Song: "Hallelujah!" *(To be sung with snapping fingers, clapping hands and tapping feet)*

Affirming Our Faith

Responsive Reading:

Reader: But it isn't easy to always give thanks to God. Sometimes life becomes boring—getting up, going to school, doing homework, goofing off.

Congregation: Nevertheless—there is meaning and possibility and new creation in every day.

Reader: Sometimes we just feel blah. We don't know the heights of gladness or the depths of agony.

Congregation: Nevertheless—there is tremendous and fascinating mystery in life and God is to glorify and enjoy.

Reader: We make so many stupid mistakes. Always doing and saying the wrong things.

Congregation: Nevertheless—God receives these things, exposes them to God's energies and offers us back new possibilities.

Reader: I don't like to read about all the things happening in the world: killings and war and sorrow.

Congregation: Nevertheless—humankind is even now being redeemed. Eternity is united with the present moment and we are a part of it.

Reader: But I'm just a child. It seems impossible for me to do anything.

Congregation: Nevertheless—God uses us to bring about eternal purposes. God has come. The Word of God has been spoken. With amazement, ecstasy, and joy we are confronted by God.

Reader: Living is an act of faith, then.

Congregation: Living means knowing and participating in the pain and agony of life, the confusions, the disappointments and the frustrations, but saying "Nevertheless"—and giving thanks.

Litany: Psalm 136 with clapping response

O give thanks unto the Lord, for He is good.

♩ ♩ ♪ ♩. ♪ ♩ ♪ ♩ ♩

Hip, hip, hooray and hallelujah.

O give thanks unto the God of gods
(Clapping response)
O give thanks to the Lord of lords
(Clapping response)
To God who alone doeth great wonders
(Clapping response)
To God that by wisdom made the heavens
(Clapping response)
To God that stretched out the earth above the waters
(Clapping response)
To God that made great lights
(Clapping response)
The sun to rule by day
(Clapping response)
The moon and stars to rule by night
(Clapping response)
O give thanks unto the God of heaven
(Clapping response)
For God's mercy endureth forever.
(Clapping response)
Yes, God's mercy endureth forever.

Recalling Our Blessings

Leader: Sometimes we do not give thanks to God because we forget God's many blessings to us. Let us use color now to remind us of the many things we have for which to thank God.

(Child comes forward carrying large sheet of yellow poster paper and stands beside leader.)

Leader: Think of all the things we have to be thankful for, that are yellow. Call out to me some of these things.

(Congregation responds with words such as: sun, buttercups, butterflies, lemon pie, flame of a candle, canaries, etc.)

(Leader gathers up these words in a simple prayer. For example: O God, we do thank thee for the sun and the buttercups, the canaries and the candles, our favorite dress and lemon pies and for the blessings you have given us that are yellow. Amen.)

(Child comes forward carrying green poster board.)

Leader: Let us think now of all the blessings we have that are green.

(Again, congregation suggests words that make up the prayer. Some examples for green are: grass, trees, pickles, moss, grapes, green beans. The same procedure is carried out for red, orange, white, and blue. Some suggestions under these colors are: red — roses, firecrackers, valentines, firetrucks, lipstick, peppermint candy; orange — marigolds, oranges, pumpkins, leaves in fall; white — snow, milk, marshmallows, lilies; blue — sky, ocean, larkspur, eyes. The group might include other colors such as black or pink. After all the blessings have been received and all the thanks have been expressed in prayer the leader says:)

Leader: Will all the children carrying poster boards come forward now? We thank you, God, who has given us so much and placed us in a rainbow world full of your blessings. Amen.

Hymn: "All Things Bright and Beautiful"

Expressing Our Thoughts

As part of our gratefulness to God we want to thank others. As we leave the service today, will each of you find someone here in our group and say "thank you" to them. It may be a teacher who has helped you, a friend who has enriched your life, a parent whose daily love we forget to say "thank you" for. Reach out to someone who has made your life better and say "thank you."

Go now with thanksgiving in your hearts and on your lips.

FIVE GRAINS OF CORN

"Five Grains of Corn" is an Old New England custom. Some families at their Thanksgiving dinner placed five grains of corn at each plate. According to one tradition this practice was started as "...a reminder of those stern days (during one of the early winters) when the corn supply of the Pilgrims was so depleted that only five grains...were rationed to each individual at a time. The Pilgrims wanted their children to remember the sacrifices, the sufferings, the hardships, which made possible the settlement... They did not want their descendants to forget. The use of five grains of corn placed by each plate was a fitting reminder of a heroic past."

Some churches like to prepare a little plastic bag of five kernels of corn attached to a 3" x 5" card with the above quotation and this statement: Why not place "the five grains" beside your plate this Thanksgiving Day as a hallowed reminder of a great sacrifice in the 1620's, as a symbol of a grateful heart today, and as a renewer of strength for days to come?

GOD PROVIDES: A THANKSGIVING WORSHIP SERVICE

by Phyllis Vos Wezeman

One of the most beautiful and beneficial Thanksgiving services I remember took place at a church my husband pastored in Muskegon Heights, Michigan. Every member of the congregation participated in a personal and powerful way.

Preparations for worship began many weeks before the fourth Thursday in November. Several Sundays prior to the holiday each member of the congregation was asked to write a petition praising or thanking God for a special blessing. These would be combined and form not only the congregational prayer, but also the outline for the service.

When the sentences were reviewed by the pastor and planning committee, they fell into two broad categories: "God provides for our physical needs" and "God provides for our spiritual needs." Therefore, the theme of the service became "God Provides." The petitions were written on transparencies and displayed on an overhead projector at appropriate times throughout the service. The two themes were explored and experienced through the use of songs and scripture passages, as well as prayer and meditations. A brief outline is provided.

Greeting
Call to Worship
Quartet: "Enter Into His Gates"
Hymn: "We Praise Thee, O God"
Invocation

GOD PROVIDES FOR OUR PHYSICAL NEEDS

Scripture: Psalm 34

THROUGH CREATION:
- Petitions expressing thanks for its beauty and majesty
- Hymn: "How Great Thou Art"

THROUGH BOUNTY:
- Petitions expressing thanks for food, the bounty of the land, gifts and blessings, and family Thanksgiving dinner
- Quartet: "Count Your Blessings"

THROUGH HEALTH:
- Petitions expressing thanks for themes ranging from recovery from illness to the miraculous working of the human body
- Hymn: "O My Soul Bless Thou Jehovah"
- Pastoral Prayer of Thanksgiving

GOD PROVIDES FOR OUR SPIRITUAL NEEDS

Scripture: Isaiah 12

THROUGH OTHERS:
- Petitions including Christian families, parents, children, friends, organizations, schools and fellowship
- Solo: "For the Beauty of the Earth"
- Hymn: "The Family of God"

THROUGH WORSHIP:
- Petitions ranging from the freedom to worship to specific programs of the congregation
- Hymn: "I Love Thy Kingdom, Lord"

THROUGH SALVATION:
- Petitions dealing with themes including the privilege of prayer, peace, Jesus' love and God's presence
- Hymn: "Thank You, Lord"
- Quartet: "To God Be The Glory"
Pastoral Prayer of Thanksgiving

Sermon
- Scripture: Colosians 4:2-4
- Message
Offering
Hymn: "Now Thank We All Our God"
Doxology

THE ORDER OF PUBLICK WORSHIP

SINGING OF A HYMN — Psalm 100

READING OF THE BIBLE

PREACHING OF THE WORD

ASKING QUESTIONS OF THE MINISTER ON THE SERMON

THE CENSURES (By officers of the Church)

THE PASTORAL PRAYER

SINGING OF A HYMN — Psalm 104

TAKING OF THE COLLECTION

ANNOUNCEMENTS

CLOSING PRAYER AND BENEDICTION (All stand)

DEPARTURE OF THE MINISTER (Remain standing)

WORSHIPING IN THE SPIRIT OF THE PILGRIMS

Historical Notes and Comments

SEATING

Men sat on the right side, women on the left side.

TYTHINGMEN AND TYTHINGWOMEN

Important in opening and closing of worship and in maintaining discipline. They kept attention focused on the worship by using a long pole with a nob at one end (for use on men) and a feather on the other end (for use on women). They signaled the beginning and end of worship by tapping with the pole. They rapped 3 times for the entrance of the minister.

BEADLE

He took the Bible from the locked "Bible Box" and preceded the minister to the pulpit.

PRAYERS

At times of prayer, all stood with arms raised above their heads. The opening prayer was 15 minutes or more. Kneeling was not acceptable because it was an "idolatrous Roman practice." "Free prayers" and not "stinted forms" were considered the

CALL TO WORSHIP
(It was customary in colonial times for a drummer to summon the congregation to worship)

ENTRANCE OF DEACONS
(All rise at signal from tythingwomen and remain standing)

ENTRANCE OF MINISTER
(Tythingwoman raps 3 times)

OPENING PRAYER OF THANKSGIVING
(All stand for prayer with hands raised above head)

SINGING

The Psalms or hymns were lined out by a Precentor or foresinger who sang out each phrase of the hymn. The people would sing it back. No organ was yet accepted by the church.

PREACHING

The sermon was regarded as the high point of the service. Sermons frequently lasted 2-4 hours. (The sermon time is mercifully shortened this morning.)

QUESTIONS

After the sermon the minister sat down and answered any questions the congregation might have regarding the sermon.

CENSURES

Officers of the church would call attention to the failures of individuals to make their conduct measure up to the expected standards.

DEPARTURE OF THE MINISTER

The congregation rose for the closing prayer and benediction and remained standing reverently until the minister departed. The minister was the last to enter and the first to leave. The Beadle took the Bible from its place on the pulpit and led the minister out. He replaced the Bible in its locked box for safekeeping.

(This service is offered by members of Pilgrim Place, a retirement community in Claremont, California for retired ministers and missionaries. They travel to churches in Southern California, usually around Thanksgiving time, and conduct this service of worship for congregations.)

most acceptable. Because of the this the Lord's Prayer was not used in worship. During the long prayers — an hour or more — people could write down the names of persons or issues for prayers, pass them to the usher, and he would carry it to the minister. People could and did say "Amens" to the portions of the prayers with which they heartily agreed or to the portions of the sermon that they wished to emphasize.

READING AND EXPOSITION OF THE SCRIPTURE

The usual practice during the Publick Worship was for the minister to read a chapter, sometimes two or three, from the Bible, explaining and interpreting as he read, for "reading without comment" was regarded as "ritualistic or dumb reading."

THANK YOU

by Robert G. Davidson

When we think of Thanksgiving we usually think of the Pilgrims and that special day they had when they celebrated and gave thanks to God for the blessings they had received. They were especially thankful for having enough food. During the previous winters they had very little food to eat. But this year was different; there was plenty of roasted turkey, clams, lobsters, fish, corn, pumpkins, and beans for everyone.

But did you know that the Pilgrims also celebrated because of their new-found friends — the Indians? They were thankful for these friends because the Indians had shown the Pilgrims how to plant and grow corn and other vegetables, so they would have enough food for the long winter. So the Pilgrims invited their new friends to share a feast with them to celebrate their many blessings.

So the Pilgrims were celebrating two things on that first Thanksgiving Day: they had enough food for the long winter and they had new friends.

As we think of Thanksgiving Day, what are the special things which we can thank God that we have? (Allow time for responses.) You have given me a long list of fine ideas, but I am thinking of three special things today which I would like you to think about.

First, let us be thankful for the food we have. All the different kinds of food we have to eat help us grow to have strong and healthy bodies. There are still children in our world who are starving and dying because they do not have enough to eat; but we are fortunate to have good meals.

Second, let us be thankful for having homes in which there are people who love us and care about the kind of person we are growing up to be. These people say in words or you see by their actions that they think you are a very important boy or girl.

Third, let us be thankful for our friends. How many friends do you have? How many new friends have you made during the past year? How important are these friends to you? What would your life be like without friends? Be thankful to God for them.

As Thanksgiving Day comes this year and we gather about the table with our families, let us take a minute or two and share how thankful we are to have plenty of food, parents and other family members who really care about us, and who give special meaning to our lives. This can become our Thanksgiving prayer to God.

THANKSGIVING WORKSHOP AND WORSHIP SERVICE

by Elaine M. Ward

On October 5, 1774 in the Town Meeting House in Cambridge, the first North American Thanksgiving proclamation was issued that did not end in "God save the king." From the time of their arrival, the Pilgrims, a religious people, set aside one day in the fall to give special thanks for the blessings of God, based on Deuteronomy 16:15. Now, in 1774, the cold war between Great Britain and her North American colonies was becoming hotter. The "Boston tea party" was only ten months old and that June Parliament had closed the port of Boston until the citizens would pay for the 10,000 pounds of tea they had dumped into the harbor. With relationships this tense, therefore, General Gage refused the request for a special day of prayer.

On October 5, the newly formed Provincial Congress met and elected John Hancock as its President. He would later become the first person to sign his name to the Declaration of Independence. Then from the small Court House they moved across the street to the Meeting House of the First Church of Cambridge.

In this proclamation the people made known their desire and need "to render Thanks to Almighty God for all the Blessings we enjoy..." Thanksgiving is the recognition of God's blessings. To "render Thanks to Almighty God for all the Blessings we enjoy," twelve centers and a worship service are suggested for a Thanksgiving Workshop.

- Share the blessings of food. Collect food the congregation has brought and display it around the altar. Discuss the problem of hunger in our world today. Jesus said, "Feed the hungry, for when you give to the hungry, you are giving to me."

- Bake bread to be used during Communion or distributed with the foods to be shared with those who have special needs.

- Read Deuteronomy 16:15 and build a "succoth" booth. Succoth or the Festival of Booths was held during harvesting, when farmers could not return home because of the amount of work required. They built tents or huts, booths called "succahs," for shelter. These booths were not meant to last long. The front was open and the other three sides were covered with tree limbs and straw. Jewish families still build succahs outside their synagogues, where they worship. Cover a pre-fabricated frame with tree branches and vegetables and fruits.

- Learn and say the fingerplay "Giving Thanks."

  We give thanks to thee, O God *(fold hands)*.
  We give thanks to thee for rain *(wiggle raise and lower fingers)*
  And sun *(make circle with arms overhead)*
  For feet that run *(run in place)*
  For you *(point to others)*,
  For me *(point to self)*,
  For everyone *(stretch arms wide)*.
  For foods that grow,
  For things to know *(point to head)*,
  To hear *(point to ears)*, and smell *(point to nose)*, and see *(point to eyes)*.
  We give thanks, O God, to thee!

- Tell the story of Jesus helping the ten lepers and discuss the blessings of health and healing.

"Help us! Please help us!" the lepers cried. Because their disease was contagious, the people had sent them out of the city, away from their families. They would leave food on a shelf in the wall that was built around the city.

Jesus was not afraid and he was sorry for the sick men. Jesus touched each of them, blessing them, and saying, "Go home, you are healed."

The men looked down at their arms and legs. They were well. They could go home to their families whom they had not seen for many years, and they ran as quickly as they could.

As the ten men ran into the city, one of them stopped suddenly. "What am I doing? I am well. Jesus has healed me!" he thought, and he ran back to thank Jesus.

"Thank you! Thank you!" he cried.

Jesus smiled. "I am glad you are well, but where are the other nine?" Then Jesus blessed the man and said, "Your trust in me has made you well. Go in peace."

16

- Prepare a cassette, creating your own music to accompany the words, "I'm thankful for the rain and sun above, for food and friends, but most of all for love!" Invite the children to sing the words in the appropriate places while viewing the filmstrip, "A Thanksgiving Feast."

- View the filmstrip "A Thanksgiving Feast."[1] A turkey, sweet potato, pumpkin, pig, and bean become friends and run away so they will not be eaten on Thanksgiving Day. In repetitive form each expresses its thanksgiving for sun and rain, friends and food and, as they share Thanksgiving together with a sharing family, most of all for love.

- Make a "blessings" collage. Have a supply of magazines, newspapers, etc. from which persons can choose pictures for their collage.

Have xeroxed copies of "I will praise you, O Lord, with all my heart..." (Psalm 138:1a) Use the collages in the worship service as litanies and to take home for family prayer.

- Draw illustrations to accompany song charts for singing hymns of Thanksgiving, such as "Praise God in the Firmament."

- Record and listen to a tape of Psalm 148. Describe God's greatness in words and pictures.

- Have paper plates and bells to make tambourines. Read Psalm 150 and praise God in sound and dance.

- Enjoy a book center with Thanksgiving books, such as:

Sometimes It's Turkey, Sometimes It's Feathers, Lorna Balian, Abingdon, Nashville, 1973. *When Mrs. Gumm finds a turkey egg, she decides to hatch it and have turkey for Thanksgiving dinner. The turkey eats the grapes, the apples, and the corn, as he grows. At last Thanksgiving Day comes and the meal is almost ready. Mrs. Gumm goes to bring her nice, plump turkey to the table...to share her feast, for as little old Mrs. Gumm said, "He'll be bigger and much plumper...next Thanksgiving."*

Cranberry Thanksgiving, Wende and Harry Devlin, Parents' Magazine Press, New York, 1971. *In this New England Thanksgiving, Maggie and her grandmother live at the edge of a cranberry bog. Each invites a guest to their simple Thanksgiving meal. Mr. Whiskers is Maggie's friend, but he smells of clams and seaweed and Grandmother is convinced he is trying to steal her secret recipe for cranberry bread. Grandmother invites Mr. Horace as* *her guest. He stays at the Town Hotel, has a gold cane and smells of lavender. When Maggie and Grandmother leave the room to clear the table after their meal, one of the men finds and steals the secret recipe, which is written at the end of the book for all to make and savor.*

Can I Help? Carol Woodard, Lutheran Church Press, Philadelphia, 1968. *Lori observes her mother cooking the turkey, her grandmother cutting the pies, her father piling wood by the fireplace, her big brother setting the table, and she wonders, "What can I do?" Finding her grandfather, Lori shares her problem and Grandfather whispers into Lori's ear how she can help. When dinner is ready, and the family seated, Grandfather asks Lori, "Are you ready?" Lori folds her hands and says the prayer before they eat, feeling happy inside because she had helped everyone to say thank you to God.*

A THANKSGIVING SERVICE OF WORSHIP

Call to Worship: "I will praise you, O Lord, with all my heart." (Ps. 138:1)

Hymn: "Praise God in the Firmament."

Thanksgiving Prayer: "Let us observe this day with reverence and with prayer that will rekindle in us the will and show us the way not only to preserve our blessings, but also to extend them to the four corners of the earth..." (from "A Thanksgiving Proclamation" by John F. Kennedy, 1961, Washington, D.C.)

Affirmation of Faith: We believe in life, in life in the Spirit, in life in communion, in life in solitude, in life in action and blessing. We believe in God, Father, Son, and Holy Spirit and in the life to come. Amen.

Litany of Thanksgiving (Use the blessing collages)

Old Testament Lesson: "I will make your name great, and you will be a blessing." Genesis 12:2a

Song: "Blessing"[2]

New Testament Lesson: Mark 10:13-16

Story: "Blessed Be God"[3]

The Shah believed in justice and mercy and each evening he would don the disguise of a dervish, a holy man, and go to the outskirts of the city to see how the poor were faring. One night he noticed

a dim light shining in a humble cottage, and hearing singing in praise of God, he went near the hut and knocked on the door, asking, "Is a stranger welcome here?"

"Come in!" cried the peasant. "A guest is the gift of God."

The peasant shared his food and drink and the two men talked late into the night. "What do you do for a living?" the Shah asked at last.

"I am a cobbler. Each day I wander through the town mending peoples' shoes. With what I earn, I buy my evening's meal."

"But what if it were forbidden to mend shoes. What would you do?"

The humble cobbler folded his hands and lifted his eyes toward heaven, saying "Blessed be God day by day."

When the Shah left, he promised to return the next evening and when he came to his palace, he proclaimed a prohibition against mending shoes without a permit. So when he approached the cobbler's hut the next night, he was surprised to hear singing in praise of God. The two men ate and the Shah asked, "What did you do today?"

"When I reached town and learned that it was prohibited to mend shoes without a permit, I carried water for the people instead. With my few pennies, I bought our bread and drink."

"What if the king prohibits carrying water?" asked the Shah.

The cobbler folded his hands and lifted his eyes towards heaven, saying, "Blessed be God day by day."

The following morning the Shah prohibited carrying water without a permit and yet when he returned to the hut of the humble cobbler that evening, he again heard singing in praise of God.

"What did you do today?" asked the Shah.

"When I learned carrying water was prohibited, I chopped wood for the people, and so we have our bread and drink."

"What if tomorrow it is prohibited to chop wood?" asked the Shah.

The humble cobbler folded his hands and lifted his eyes toward heaven, saying, "Blessed be God day by day."

The following morning all woodchoppers were recruited into the king's guard. The cobbler was given a sword, but that evening, having earned no money, he pawned the steel blade from his sword, bought his food, and returned home. There he made himself a wooden blade and put it in his sheath. When the king came, he again heard singing in praise of God.

The cobbler told him what he had done and the Shah asked, "What will happen if there is a sword inspection tomorrow?"

The cobbler folded his hands before him and lifted his eyes toward heaven, saying, "Blessed be God day by day."

The following morning the chief officer called to the cobbler. "This prisoner has been sentenced to death and you are ordered to behead him."

"I will not! I have never killed a man," the cobbler protested.

"If you do not, you will be beheaded!"

The cobbler, clasping the hilt of his sword in one hand and the sheath in the other, cried before the assembled crowd, raising his eyes toward heaven, "Almighty God, you know that I would not take the life of an innocent man. If this man be guilty, let my sword be of steel, but if he is innocent, let it be turned to wood."

So saying, the cobbler drew the sword from his sheath and...behold...it was of wood! The crowd stared in amazement and the Shah revealed his identity, hugging and kissing his friend, and appointing him a court advisor, for the Shah had learned from the humble cobbler...blessed be God day by day.

Hymn: "Blest Be the Tie That Binds."

Benediction: Go now in thanksgiving with God's blessing. In Christ's name. Amen.

[1] "The Thanksgiving Feast." Elaine Ward, Allen, Texas: Tabor Publications, 1981. The filmstrip is also available in storybook.

[2] **Songs For Young Children.** Mary Lu Walker, N.Y.: Paulist Press, 1973.

[3] **Folktales of Israel** (adapted and retold). Dov Noy, Chicago: University of Chicago Press, 1963.

A SERVICE OF THANKS-SINGING

by Phyllis Vos Wezeman

The Psalms are filled with phrases which tell God's people to sing His praises. "Sing to the Lord with thanksgiving," from Psalm 147, "Sing to the Lord a new song," found in Psalm 149 and the familiar words of Psalm 100, "Serve the Lord with gladness; come before him with joyful songs," are only a few examples.

One year worshippers in the community of Mishawaka, Indiana came together under the sponsorship of the United Religious Community, an interfaith partnership of congregations in the county, and the local ministerial association, for a Thanks-singing Hymnfest. Familiar songs of praise as well as new hymns of harvest were interspersed with scripture readings and offered to God in thanks for His great gifts. A combined choir representing several area churches participated. An outline of the service follows.

WELCOME
PRELUDE
OPENING HYMN: "Come, Ye Thankful People, Come"
    Stanza One: Choir
    Remaining Stanzas: All

HYMN OF PRAISE: "All People That on Earth Do Dwell"
    Tune: Old Hundredth
    Stanza Four: Unison
RESPONSIVE HYMN: "We Plow the Fields" (Tune: Dresden)
    Minister:
    We plow the fields, and scatter
    The good seed on the land,
    But it is fed and watered
    By God's almighty hand;
    He sends the snow in winter,
    The warmth to swell the grain,
    The breezes and the sunshine,
    And soft refreshing rain.
    All sing:
    All good gifts around us
    Are sent from heaven above;
    Then thank the Lord,
    O thank the Lord for all His love.
    Minister:
    He only is the Maker
    Of all things near and far;
    He paints the wayside flower,
    He lights the evening star;
    The winds and waves obey Him,
    By Him the birds are fed;
    Much more to us, His children,
    He gives our daily bread.
    All sing:
    All good gifts around us

Are sent from heaven above;
Then thank the Lord,
O thank the Lord, for all His love.
Minister:
We thank Thee, then, O Father,
For all things bright and good,
The seedtime and the harvest,
Our life, our health, our food;
Accept the gifts we offer,
For all thy love imparts,
And what Thou most desirest,
Our humble, thankful hearts.
All sing:
All good gifts around us
Are sent from heaven above;
Then thank the Lord,
O thank the Lord for all His love.
HYMN OF THANKS: "Now Thank We all Our God"
SCRIPTURE LESSONS
Psalm 67
Luke 17:11-19
NEW HYMN OF HARVEST
"As Saints of Old"
Tune: Regwal
Text: Frank von Christierson, 1961
Stanza One: Choir
Stanzas Two and Three: All
PRAYER
Leader:
Not alone for mighty empire
Stretching far o'er land and sea,
Not alone for bounteous harvests
Do we praise you gratefully
People:
Standing in the living present,
Memory and hope between,
Lord, we would with deep thanksgiving
Praise you most for things unseen.
Leader:
Not for battleship and fortress,
Not for conquests of the sword,
But for conquests of the spirit
We give thanks to you, O Lord;
People:
For the heritage of freedom,
For the home, the church, the school.
For the open door to justice
In a land the people rule.
Leader:
For the armies of the faithful,
Those who past and left no name;
For the glory that illumines
Patriot lives of deathless fame;
People:
For our prophets and apostles,
Loyal to the living Word;
For the strong and free in spirit

We give thanks to you, O Lord.
Leader:
God of justice, save the people
From the clash of race and creed;
From the strife of class and faction,
Make our nation free indeed.
People:
Keep its faith in simple justice
Strong as when its life began,
Till it find complete fruition
By the guiding of your hand.
THANKSGIVING OFFERING
Offertory: "Now Thank We all Our God"
Congregational Response: "We Give Thee But Thine Own"
Prayer of Dedication
CLOSING HYMN: "All Praise to Thee, My God, This Night"
BENEDICTION
POSTLUDE

A THANKSGIVING WORSHIP SERVICE FOR CHILDREN

by Elaine M. Ward

Thanksgiving is a time for giving thanks. Thanksgiving is our secular and sacred holiday in which we give thanks. To give thanks is to be glad, grateful, to count of our blessings, and to express that gratitude to the One who gives.

One of the greatest gifts of God is Creation. That this world should be here with birds and beasts, light and dark, food and shelter and people, especially people, is unbelievable without a Creator. That this world should be dependable, day follows night, death follows birth, is unbelievable without a Planner.

So we sing our thanks and remember our stories of thanksgiving and of creation.

CALL TO WORSHIP

"This is the day which the Lord has made. Let us rejoice and be glad in it." (Psalm 118:24)

Processional Hymn: "Now Thank We All Our God"

Special Music: Child Soloist or Children's Choir

A Psalm of Praise (Each line to be read by a different person)

Praise the Lord...Praise, God, sun and moon,
Praise God, all you shining stars.
Praise God, you highest heavens...
Praise the Lord from the earth,
you sea creatures and all ocean depths,
lightning and hail, snow and clouds,
stormy winds that do his bidding,
you mountains and all hills,
fruit trees and all cedars,
wild animals and all cattle,
small creatures and flying birds,
kings of the earth and all nations,
Praise the Lord!

OLD TESTAMENT READING:

Psalm 19:1: "The heavens declare the glory of God; the skies proclaim the work of his hands."

The psalmist sang praises for the beauties of the earth. Look around. See and smell, taste and touch, and hear the earth and sky praise God's creation.

Hymn: "Come, Ye Thankful People, Come"

NEW TESTAMENT READING:

Luke 12:22-24, 27

A Thanksgiving Story[1]

Once upon a time there was a girl who did not know what Thanksgiving was, but since there was a special day to celebrate it, she decided the best way to find out what Thanksgiving was would be to go out and find one. As she walked, she heard a dog bark and then a painful howl. Following the sound she found the dog whose paw was caught in a trap.

"Let me help you," said the girl, releasing the dog's foot from the trap.

"Thank you," barked the dog and when the girl had comforted the dog, he asked, "Where are you going?"

"I am going to find Thanksgiving," she replied.

"What on earth is Thanksgiving?" asked the dog. "Is it hard as a bone? Sweet as a biscuit? Warm as a home? What is Thanksgiving?"

"I do not know, but come along with me and we shall see," she said.

The girl and the dog walked along until they came to a farm. There they saw a very sad cow. "What is the matter, sad cow?" they asked.

"No one has milked me for two days," said the sad cow.

"Let me help you," she replied, finding a bucket and milking the cow.

"Thank you," mooed the cow and when the girl had comforted the cow, the cow asked, "Where are you going?"

"We are going to find Thanksgiving," they replied.

"What is Thanksgiving? Is it as tasty as grass? Refreshing as water? Warm as a barn? What is

Thanksgiving?" asked the cow.

"We do not know but come along and we will see," they said.

The girl and the dog and the cow walked along until they came to a horse, a very angry horse. "What is the matter, angry horse?" they asked.

"My master has tied me to this tree to take me to market tomorrow and sell me."

"Let me help you," said the girl, untying the horse from the tree.

"Thank you," neighed the horse and when the girl had comforted the horse, the horse asked, "Where are you going?"

"We are going to find Thanksgiving," they replied.

"What is Thanksgiving? Is it as soft as the wind across my back? As sweet as the song of the birds in the morning? Free as a sunfilled field? What is Thanksgiving?"

"We do not know but come along with us and we shall see," they said.

The girl and the dog and the cow and the horse walked along until they came to a very fat pumpkin in the field, crying, "What is the matter, crying pumpkin?" they asked.

"Tomorrow I am to be made into pumpkin pie and be eaten..."

"Let me help you," said the girl, pulling off the pumpkin from the vine.

"Thank you," said the pumpkin and when the girl had comforted the pumpkin, it asked, "Where are you going?"

"We are going to find Thanksgiving," they replied.

"What is Thanksgiving? Is it as dark as a quiet night? As wet as soft raindrops? Warm as the sunshine? What is Thanksgiving?"

"We do not know but come along with us and we shall see," they said.

The girl and the dog and the cow and the horse

and the pumpkin walked along until they came to a deserted farmhouse.

"I am thankful you set me free from the trap," said the dog, "but I am tired and hungry and think I will stay here."

"I am thankful you gave me comfort and love," said the cow, "but I am tired and hungry and think I will stay here."

"I am thankful you gave me my freedom," said the horse, "but I am tired and hungry and think I will stay here."

"I am thankful you gave me new friends," said the pumpkin, "but I am tired and hungry and think I will stay here."

"And thank you, all of you, for going with me on our journey, but I am tired and hungry and think I will return home," said the girl.

And she did, and when she came near she could hear the happy singing and smell the food cooking and see the smoke rising from the chimney, and when she opened the door she felt warm all through and through, and began to sing her thanks to God, for she had found Thanksgiving.

LITANY OF THANKSGIVING:

Leader: Now let us too find Thanksgiving and give our thanks to God. (Invite the children to express the things that make them glad, and after each, say together: "We thank you, God.")

A THANKSGIVING PRAYER

Dear God, put the song of thanksgiving into our hearts,
So we may live lovingly all our days,
Showing Your love and singing Your praise. Amen.

Hymn: "Doxology"

BENEDICTION:

Now blessed by God's gifts and presence go out among others to care for God's creation and for one another, in Christ's name. Amen.

---

[1]Based on Trina Schart Hyman's children's story, "How Six Found Christmas."

STORIES, POEMS, AND PLAYS

PARABLE FOR THANKSGIVING

by Janice Bacon

It happened once upon a time, a long time ago, the Spirit of Thanksgiving said, "It's time for me to know what people down below on Earth are thankful for this year. So I must go down and ask them if I really want to find out."

Well, the Spirit flew down to the town near by and said, "I guess it's only right to try the richest man first, because surely he will be the most thankful person I'd ever want to see."

The Rich Man was eating his lunch that day and Spirit could see he had no time to play. He ate very quickly with a frown on his face. He worked all the time he sat at his place.

The Spirit said, "Sir, for what do you give thanks?"

"Look! I've no time today because all of my banks are causing me to have a great deal of worry. That's why I have to eat my lunch in a hurry. People try to rob me, to take all my money; being rich is work, and it's not very funny!"

Spirit could see that the Rich Man was sad. Not being thankful can make one feel bad. So, Spirit left the Seeds of Thankfulness that day. He smiled a sad smile and flew on his way.

Next he found his way to an artist's studio where a very famous artist had paintings out to show. She was almost in tears, she was so upset. She said, "Look at this picture, the paint is still wet! I went a long way to find a perfect place to capture a perfect rainbow to paint in this space. Now look at this painting," the poor artist said, "the blue is too blue and the red is too red."

To Spirit the rainbow was as perfect as could be; why she was so upset was more than he could see. To him the rainbow looked like Nature's very own, but the artist turned away with yet another groan. The Spirit of Thanksgiving thought he'd better not ask if she were thankful and, if so, for what. So he left his Seeds of Thanksgiving near the artist's brush and without another word, he left in a rush.

Next he stopped to see a Mighty Muscle Man whose arms were as strong as polished steel bands. "Excuse me, sir, can you say what you're thankful for today?"

"No! I've no time to be thankful and I wish you'd go away! My muscles are aging and I must work every hour to keep up my mighty strength and power."

So Spirit, very sadly, left the Seeds on the floor, and spreading his wings, flew out the door.

"I never thought it would take this long to find someone singing a Thanksgiving Song. Is there no one on Earth thankful this year? If someone is out there I wish he would appear!"

Not expecting a great deal more Spirit approached and knocked at the door of a small neat home. When the door opened up he could hear laughing children playing with a pup. Spirit was excited, he knew that sound! It meant that happiness was all around!

He asked the Mother, "What's the secret here? What will you be giving thanks for this year?"

The Mother answered with a smile on her face as she looked around with pleasure at her place; "We haven't much money but we have good health. Our love for each other is our greatest wealth. Our friends surround us when we have a need and, in return, we plant a Thankfulness Seed!"

Spirit was happy! He knew the truth. Thanksgiving was alive! He had the proof! So he picked up his Seeds and in his heart was a song—Thanksgiving on Earth was still going strong!

Spirit left a message for each of us that day: "Plant the Seeds of Thankfulness and I'll never go away!"

HILARY'S THANKSGIVING

by Elaine Ward

"We're going to have turkey and dressing and sweet potatoes and pumpkin pie," Alice replied to her teacher's question, "What will you eat on Thanksgiving?"

All of the children chimed in, "Me, too! Me, too!" Everyone that is, but Hilary. The teacher noticed Hilary was silent and sad and then she remembered that Hilary's father had lost his job several months earlier and still was not working.

"Why don't I learn not to ask questions like that?" thought Mrs. Arp, quickly adding aloud, "It's not what we eat on Thanksgiving, however, that is important, but how thankful we are to God for whatever we have."

It was too late. The damage had been done. She could see the hurt in Hilary's eyes. "In some parts of the world the children are always hungry. Boys and girls, there are children who are starving in our world today," she continued.

Hilary knew that she would have food on Thanksgiving, even if it wasn't turkey, but somehow knowing that others were hungry did not help the hurt right now. It was knowing that she had so little that seemed to matter most with Hilary.

"Could we collect food for the hungry in our city?" Bart asked his teacher.

"What do the rest of you think?" Mrs. Arp asked the class.

All of the boys and girls, including Hilary, thought it was a good idea, and all the way home that Sunday Hilary wondered what she could bring to share.

When Hilary told her mother, Mother frowned. "I know we have more than many, Hilary, but right now there isn't anything we can afford to give away."

"Mother, may I babysit after school for the twins? I could earn some money. Only until Thanksgiving? Please?"

Mother agreed at last, when Hilary promised she would not be too tired to do her homework each night.

Hilary enjoyed playing with the twins, but it was work keeping up with two two-year-olds. Each night she could barely stay awake to do her homework, but she did, for a promise was a promise to be kept.

The Sunday before Thanksgiving Hilary could hardly carry her bag of groceries to church, they were so heavy.

Mrs. Arp looked at the bag and gasped. "You didn't need to bring so much, Hilary!"

"I wanted to, and besides I earned the money myself, taking care of the twins," Hilary replied.

Each child brought a can or a box of some food to share, but no one had thought of bringing as much as Hilary brought. She wasn't trying to show-off or outdo the others. It was only that Hilary knew how it felt to be hungry.

Looking at the food stacked in the box, Hilary suddenly didn't mind that she would not have turkey and all the special Thanksgiving foods that year. There were many different kinds of hungers and Hilary suddenly felt well-fed, if not "stuffed."

TO THINK ABOUT

Why did Hilary feel "stuffed?"

What other kinds of "hunger" are there besides food hunger?

Have you ever been hungry for attention, or love, or being part of a group, or being able to help others?

Do you know anyone out of work? Is being poor Hilary's fault?

How do you treat people who are different from you? Think about a particular person who is different. How do you relate to that person?

A TIME OF THANKSGIVING

by Neil C. Fitzgerald

CHARACTERS:
Mrs. Martin, mother
Mr. Martin, father
Julie, daughter, ten years old
Lisa, narrator
Peter, John Alden
Billy, Squanto
Mary, Priscilla Mullins
Greg, Governor William Bradford
Doug, Elder William Brewster
Hank, Captain Myles Standish

TIME: Late afternoon.

SETTING: The Martin living room. A sofa stands in the middle of the room flanked by two end tables. An easy chair is also on each side of the sofa. Door on left leads outside. Door on right leads to the rest of the house.

AT RISE: JULIE, wearing pajamas and covered loosely by a blanket, is asleep on the sofa, MRS. MARTIN enters from right and pulls the blanket up over JULIE. MR. MARTIN enters from right and moves to the front of the stage. MRS. MARTIN joins him.

MRS. MARTIN: Where are you going?

MR. MARTIN: To have Julie's medicine refilled.

MRS. MARTIN: I'm really worried about her.

MR. MARTIN: Didn't the doctor say she was coming along fine?

MRS. MARTIN: Physically yes. But, like me, he is concerned that she hasn't perked up and started to take an interest in things.

MR. MARTIN: Maybe she just needs more time.

MRS. MARTIN: Maybe.

MR. MARTIN: Did you call the school?

MRS. MARTIN: Yes. Miss Quinn is sending her books and assignments over. She also said she is sending a surprise for Julie.

MR. MARTIN: Well, I'd better get going. *(MR. MARTIN exits left.)*

JULIE *(Awakened by the door closing)***:** Was that Daddy leaving?

MRS. MARTIN: Yes, he went to get your medicine.

JULIE: Mom, I hate that stuff.

MRS. MARTIN: I know, but it will help you get better.

JULIE: I don't feel any better.

MRS. MARTIN: Julie, tell me, what's bothering you?

JULIE: Everything. I can't be with my friends. I'm going to miss the play at school. Most of all we're not going to be able to visit Grandma this Thanksgiving.

MRS. MARTIN: She will miss you.

JULIE: And so will all the rest of the family.

MRS. MARTIN: Yes.

JULIE: And it's all my fault.

MRS. MARTIN: Stop talking like that. You couldn't help what happened.

JULIE: I can just picture everyone sitting down around the dining room table with the turkey set before Uncle Jim. Ther'll be potatoes and gravy and squash and cranberry sauce. And for dessert Grandma's delicious pumpkin pie. And after the meal all the kids in the family will play games outside. Oh, Mom, I feel so awful.

MRS. MARTIN: Julie, you mustn't – (Doorbell rings. MRS. MARTIN walks across the room and opens the door.) Lisa!

LISA: Hi, Mrs. Martin. I've brought Julie's books.

MRS. MARTIN: Well, come in. (LISA enters carrying school books followed by PETER carrying a wooden hammer, BILLY wearing a headband with a feather, MARY wearing a Pilgrim bonnet, GREG wearing a Pilgrim hat, DOUG wearing a Pilgrim hat and carrying a Bible, and HANK wearing a soldier's helmet and carrying a sword.)

ALL: Hi, Julie.

JULIE: Hi, guys.

LISA: Julie, I brought all your work. Miss Quinn said to tell you the assignments are on papers in each book and if you have trouble to call her.

JULIE: Thanks, Lisa.

LISA: Also, Miss Quinn thought that since you won't be able to see the school play, we leading players could show you a shortened version, if that is okay, Mrs. Martin.

MRS. MARTIN: Julie, what do you think?

JULIE: I'd love it!

MRS. MARTIN: Well, I've got a dinner to prepare. But I'll sneak a peek whenever I can. (MRS. MARTIN exits right, but occasionally reappears to look in on what's going on.)

LISA: All right, everyone line up. (Pupils form a line at one end of the sofa. LISA stands at the other end facing both JULIE and the audience.) Parents, teachers, friends, we have gathered together this day to tell you the story of the Pilgrims coming to America and about the first Thanksgiving. Of course, the Pilgrims did not call themselves pilgrims. At that time they were called Separatists. But before we begin, I want you to meet our leading players.

PETER: My name is John Alden. I am a cooper. I make barrels and other things for the Pilgrims.

BILLY: I'm Squanto. I am an Indian. I was captured by English explorers and brought as a slave to England. That's how I learned English. I was able to return to America in time to help the Pilgrims.

MARY: My name is Priscilla Mullins. I am in love with John Alden and plan to marry him.

GREG: My name is William Bradford. I was elected Governor of Plymouth Plantation but not until Governor John Carver died in the Spring of 1621.

DOUG: I'm Elder William Brewster. I helped lead the Pilgrims from Scoorby in England to Leyden in Holland and finally to America. I conduct the religious services for the Pilgrims.

HANK: I'm Captain Miles Standish. I was hired to see that the Pilgrims are kept safe from all harm.

LISA: Julie, there are more people in the play, but Miss Quinn said we were enough to send.

JULIE: I understand.

LISA: Now the Pilgrims arrived from England aboard the Mayflower in November of 1620.

HANK (Pointing toward audience): Land ho!

LISA: The ship anchored off Provincetown at the tip of Cape Cod. A landing party was sent ashore in a longboat. (HANK, PETER, GREG, and DOUG pretend to be sitting in a boat rowing.) But the longboat couldn't reach the shore so the men had to wade ashore. (The boys pretend to step from the boat and wade ashore.) The men were anxious to meet any inhabitants but saw not even a sign of Indians. So they filled the boat with juniper and returned to the Mayflower.

PETER: Should we row back, Lisa?

LISA: No, we'll skip that part. The next day, a Sunday, was the Lord's Day and the Pilgrims observed it in their customary way.

DOUG (With all gathered around him except BILLY, opens the Bible): "The Lord is your guardian; the Lord is your shade; He is beside you at your right hand. The sun shall not harm you by day, nor the moon at night."

LISA: The next day the Pilgrims went ashore to refresh themselves and the women to wash their clothes. *(MARY kneels and pretends to be washing clothes.)* Thus did Monday washday become a longtime New England tradition. The Pilgrims continued to go ashore. Finally one day they saw some Indians.

BILLY: Julie, I'm going to play the Indians' part although Squanto didn't meet the Pilgrims until much later.

JULIE: Right.

LISA: Anyway, the Pilgrims spotted the Indians and ran after them hoping to talk to them. *(Boys chase BILLY around the sofa much to JULIE'S delight.)* But the Pilgrims couldn't catch the Indians. However, on one of their trips ashore the Pilgrims discovered a cache of Indian corn that had been buried. *(Boys kneel and pretend to be digging.)* The food was to help the Pilgrims make it through the winter.

GREG: Lisa, we'd better get on to Plymouth.

LISA: Okay. The Pilgrims decided not to stay on the outer cape so they sailed into Plymouth Harbor. There they went ashore stepping onto a giant rock. *(HANK pretends to step out of the longboat and help MARY step onto the rock.)* Today the rock is called Plymouth Rock.

JULIE: My Grandma has seen Plymouth Rock.

LISA: The first winter was terrible. Nearly half of the Pilgrims died. *(All except BILLY stand in a straight line with heads bowed.)*

DOUG *(Again from the Bible)*: "The breakers of death surged round about me, the destroying floods overwhelmed me. The Lord rewarded me according to justice; for I kept the ways of the Lord and was not disloyal to my God."

LISA: With the spring came hope. Squanto returned to Plymouth for this land had been his home, the home of his people the Patuxets who had been wiped out by a plague. Squanto decided to stay and help the Pilgrims. One day he brought some herring to the plantation. *(BILLY pretends to hold a string of fish. He kneels. The others gather round.)*

GREG: Squanto, are you going to cook those fish?

BILLY: No.

PETER: What then?

BILLY: You will see.

DOUG: Look, he plants the fish and now he plants the corn in mounds above the fish.

BILLY: Now you must guard against the wolves for they will be drawn here by the smell of the fish.

GREG: Squanto, you are a special instrument sent by God for our good.

LISA: And as Governor Bradford recorded in his history of Plymouth Plantation, without the corn they might have starved. In the fall the Pilgrims had a good harvest.

DOUG *(Again from the Bible)*: "Give thanks to the Lord, for He is good, for His kindness endures forever!"

GREG: We have truly been blessed.

HANK: We have cod and bass and other fish.

PETER: And wild turkeys and venison.

DOUG: And waterfowl.

MARY: And corn meal.

GREG: We shall have a feast. Squanto, go and tell your great sachem Massasoit he is most welcome.

LISA: So it was that the food was prepared. *(All busy themselves pretending to set up the great feast.)* There was enough for three days of feasting. The time of this first Thanksgiving, most believe, was during October of 1621. Massasoit arrived with ninety Indians. They were carrying five deer that they had killed. *(Pause)* Julie, Matt Burgess is our Massasoit, but he was out sick today.

HANK: But it doesn't really matter because he doesn't have any lines.

DOUG: Julie, just pretend Massasoit is coming from behind the sofa.

JULIE *(Jumping up and wrapping the blanket around her)*: Well, if he doesn't have any lines, I'll be

Massasoit. Just tell me what to do. *(Runs around behind the sofa.)*

MARY: Julie, maybe you shouldn't do this.

JULIE: I feel fine, really.

LISA: Governor Bradford stepped forward to greet the great chief. *(GREG and JULIE start toward each other.)*

MRS. MARTIN *(Enters right)*: Julie Martin! *(JULIE scampers back onto the sofa.)*

MARY: Mrs. Martin, I told her she shouldn't—

MRS. MARTIN: It's okay, Mary.

LISA: Anyway, the play ends with everyone eating and having a good time.

PETER: I guess we should be going.

JULIE: Thanks, guys, for coming. You were great.

HANK: We hope you'll be back in school really quick, Julie.

MRS. MARTIN: The doctor said maybe before Christmas.

DOUG: Great! *(All the pupils start to leave.)*

JULIE: Bye and thanks again.

ALL: Bye, Julie. *(Pupils exit and MR. MARTIN enters left.)*

MR. MARTIN: What have I missed?

MRS. MARTIN: A preview of the school's Thanksgiving play.

JULIE: And I got to be Massasoit until Mom caught me.

MR. MARTIN: I brought your medicine.

MRS. MARTIN: Well, I'd say your daughter just had some very good medicine.

JULIE: Mom, Dad, I'm sorry. I guess missing out on everything made me feel really sorry for myself. I was miserable and made you feel the same way. During the play I realized how much I have to be thankful for. I have you, Grandma, all the family, wonderful friends, a good home, a good school, plenty to eat—I could go on and on. The Pilgrims had so little.

MR. MARTIN: Most importantly, Julie, they had their faith in God.

JULIE: I'll remember that when I say my prayers tonight.

MRS. MARTIN *(Hugging JULIE)*: You're definitely on the way to recovery. Now I've got a dinner to finish.

MR. MARTIN: Need any help?

MRS. MARTIN: As a matter of fact I do. *(Picks up Julie's school books and hands them to JULIE)* Here, this ought to keep you busy.

JULIE: Homework. Ugh! It's hard to be thankful for homework. *(MR. & MRS. MARTIN exit right. JULIE opens a book and begins to read. CURTAIN)*

PRODUCTION NOTES

Characters: 6 male, 4 female.

Playing Time: 13 minutes.

Costumes: Everyday dress.

Properties: Two Pilgrim hats, Pilgrim bonnet, soldier's helmet, headband with feather, wooden hammer, sword, Bible, blanket, school books.

Setting: Living room with sofa, two end tables and two easy chairs. Exits to stage left and right.

Lighting: No special effects.

Sound: Doorbell.

THANKSGIVING IN NEW ENGLAND

by Elaine Ward

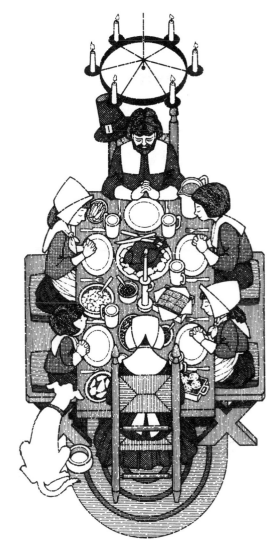

Once a long time ago, on Thanksgiving Day in New England, two pilgrim girls were alone in their home.

"The snow is too deep for you to come with us," said their father. "Your mother and I will be home from church shortly."

"Remember the turkey," her mother cried over her shoulder as she disappeared into the wilderness.

The door was bolted as Priscilla sighed. "I wish I could have gone. Perhaps I would have seen an Indian."

"Don't talk that way, Priscilla, and come away from the window," said Sara, her older sister. "Indians hate the white people."

"Black Eagle didn't," Priscilla protested.

Chief Black Eagle had been their friend, but he had moved deeper into the woods with his family that early fall.

Priscilla stood by the window, staring at the white snow filled with tracks of deer and rabbit and of her parents who had gone to church. Suddenly she held her breath. Her wish had happened sooner than she realized. Outside the door a small Indian boy looked up at Priscilla.

Priscilla ran to the door and invited the boy to come in out of the cold. The small boy hesitated and then shivered, and seeing the warm fireplace, and smelling the baking turkey, he came in and sat down by the fireplace, watching warily out of his right eye.

"Priscilla, I do believe he is hungry," said Sara. "Some of the food is ready."

Sara dished some of the food onto a plate and handed it to the boy with a smile. He eagerly ate the food and no sooner had he eaten than he lay down by the fire and fell asleep. The fire made the room warm, and the girls quickly fell asleep, as well.

Imagine Priscilla's surprise when she awoke to see two Indians towering over her. She was about to scream, when she saw Mother and Father standing with them.

One of the Indians was Black Feather, and he was telling her father how Priscilla had stopped a fight by feeding and then befriending the son of the other Indian, Chief Red Arrow, standing beside him.

"If you come in peace now, come and share our Thanksgiving feast!" Father said to the two men.

From that Thanksgiving on everyone spoke of how Priscilla brought peace to the forest by her love and through her sharing.

31

PASTOR TIMOTHY TINKER'S TURKEY

by Jane K. Priewe

Since this activity includes your audience, divide the youngsters into small groups and assign each group a sound to make when their word is read. Words or names have been underlined in the story so the reader will know to hesitate while special groups make appropriate sounds.

Pastor Timothy Tinker—loud sigh
Tina Tinker—Oh, my goodness!
Fourth of July—bang, boom, pop
turkey—gobble, gobble, gobble,
cat—meow, meow
hen—cackle, cackle
rickety car—chuga, chuga, chuga
little girl—clap hands

Pastor Timothy Tinker was sad. Thanksgiving Day was nearly here and he still hadn't figured out what his congregation could do for the poor people in Townson.

"Tomorrow is Thanksgiving Day," Pastor Tim's wife, Tina, said one morning. "Stir yourself, Tim Tinker, and go kill our turkey, so I can roast it."

Armed with a hatchet, Pastor Tim ambled toward the hen yard where he saw the turkey strutting around. When he finally reached the hen yard, the turkey had wandered into a nearby shed.

"Timothy!" Tina called from the back porch. "Get a move on! I want that turkey for Thanksgiving dinner, not the Fourth of July!"

"I'll get him, Tina." Pastor Tim strolled into the shed. It was very quiet until a cat spied the turkey on top of a feed bin. The cat chased the turkey right between Pastor Tim's legs.

The turkey escaped over a wire fence, and flapped to the hood of Pastor Tinker's rickety car.

Pastor Tim jogged toward the car, but the turkey flopped off the hood and scurried down the road toward Townson.

"Drat that two-winged critter!" Pastor Timothy Tinker sputtered. "If I lose that bird, Tina will be madder than a wet hen!"

He climbed into his rickety car, and rattled along to town. When he arrived, the turkey was nowhere in sight. Pastor Timothy cruised up and down streets, calling to people if they'd seen his turkey. Nobody had.

Finally, he gave up, and started for home. Pastor Tim didn't drive very fast, because he knew Tina would be angry. Then, just coming around a corner, he saw a little girl carrying the turkey under her arm.

The pastor made a squeaky stop, and asked kindly, "Where are you going with that turkey, little girl?"

"I'm taking it home to my mother," she smiled brightly. "We've never had a turkey, and this one came right up to me on the street."

"Enjoy your Thanksgiving!" Pastor Timothy Tinker waved, and chugged out of town. At home he told Tina Tinker what had happened to the turkey. Beaming at his wife, he added, "And I had a wonderful idea for our congregation on the way home. Here's what we'll do."

Thanksgiving Day dawned crisp and clear. The congregation at Pastor Timothy Tinker's church arrived in Townson with their cooked dinners. They set up tables and shared their meals with the poor and anyone else who wanted to join them.

Tina Tinker squeezed her husband's hand under the table. "You've made this the best Thanksgiving Day, Timothy Tinker—for all of us, but mostly for that happy, little girl!"

CRANBERRY SAUCE

by Robert B. Ward

Characters: Man, Woman, Policeman, Fireman, Nurse, Repairman, Mrs. Scoby

Scene: A living room in a modern home. As the skit begins the man and woman are on opposite sides of the room. They are angry with one another. They walk toward each other and pass without speaking. They turn and walk past each other again. As they turn back the second time the woman speaks with disgust.

Woman: Men!

Man: Well, go ahead and say it.

(They cross silently, then turn.)

Woman: Say what?

Man: Confess my sins for me, that's what. Tell me I'm stupid.

Woman: It's obvious.

Man: I still say it doesn't matter.

Woman: Doesn't matter? Doesn't matter. This is Thanksgiving Day and you say it doesn't matter?

Man: Of course not. So I forgot the cranberry sauce. We can have Thanksgiving without cranberry sauce. The main thing is to be thankful.

(Couple continue to walk back and forth.)

Woman: Huh! I should be thankful for a forgetful husband?

Man: How about a nagging wife?

Woman: You know that I don't na... *(Pauses to change the subject.)* Well, it is Thanksgiving Day. Let's just open the door and let a little Thanksgiving in. *(Opens door, jumps back gasping as policeman enters.)*

Woman: Oh, my! Who are you?

Policeman: *(Laughing at woman's alarm.)* It's all right ma'am. I'm Thanksgiving. You said you were going to open the door and let a little Thanksgiving in. *(Walks across the stage toward the man who draws back.)* Well, here I am.

Man: I didn't do anything. Just forgot to get the cranberry sauce. That's no crime at all.

Woman: Thanksgiving? A Policeman?

(Enter Fireman and Nurse.)

Nurse: And a Fireman and a Nurse.

Fireman: The man from the power company is outside.

Policeman: We are all a part of your Thanksgiving.

(Repairman enters.)

Repairman: All of us are working today.

Woman: On Thanksgiving?

Fireman: Sometimes it is a very busy day.

Man: I bet that if you have a fire you don't have cranberry sauce.

Fireman: Oh yes! We cook

our own meals at the fire station — turkey, dressing, sauce and everything. It would be un-American not to have cranberry sauce!

Nurse: Oh, I wouldn't say that! We have plenty of people on I.V.'s today. But someone is caring for them. That's part of Thanksgiving.

Man: And you might say that all of you are caring for us. Each one of you is working so we might have a better Thanksgiving.

Repairman: I have to go now. I have a call from the powerhouse. I'm glad you asked us to stop by.

Nurse: Me too. Oh, here comes someone else.

(Nurse and repairman exit. Enter Mrs. Scoby.)

Woman: This is Mrs. Scoby, our neighbor.

Policeman: Yes ma'am. Glad to meet you. Sorry I have to go.

Fireman: Me too.

(Fireman and Policeman exit.)

(Continued on page 34)

THE BEST THANKSGIVING

by Elaine Ward

One crisp and cold November day a chicken found a kernel of corn.

"If you will come and be my guest, my Thanksgiving will be truly blest," cheeped the chicken to his friend, the bird.

"I will gladly be your guest, if you will share my worm with all the rest," sang the bird.

Then the chicken and the bird invited the squirrel to their Thanksgiving feast. "I will gladly be your guest, if you will share my nuts with all the rest," chattered the squirrel.

Then the chicken and the bird and the squirrel invited the rat to their Thanksgiving feast. "I will gladly be your guest, if you will share my cheese with all the rest," squeaked the rat.

Then the chicken and the bird and the squirrel and the rat invited the cat to their Thanksgiving feast.

"I will gladly be your guest, if you will share my milk with all the rest," purred the cat.

Then the chicken and the bird and the squirrel and the rat and the cat invited the rabbit to their Thanksgiving feast.

"I will gladly be your guest, if you will share my carrots with all the rest," wiggled the rabbit.

Then the chicken and the bird and the squirrel and the rat and the cat and the rabbit invited the pig to their Thanksgiving feast.

"I will gladly be your guest, if you will share my leftovers with all the rest," oinked the pig.

Then the chicken and the bird and the squirrel and the rat and the cat and the rabbit and the pig invited the dog to their Thanksgiving feast.

"I will gladly be your guest, if you will share my bone with all the rest," barked the dog.

On that Thanksgiving Day all the animals agreed, "This Thanksgiving is the best, because we shared with all the rest!"

CRANBERRY SAUCE
(Continued from page 33)

Mrs. Scoby: Who were they? What was that all about?

Man: We opened the door to let in Thanksgiving, and there they were.

Mrs. Scoby: Oh, that's what I came for—Thanksgiving.

Man: Well, you came to the right place.

Mrs. Scoby: I need to borrow some sauce. You know Thanksgiving is cranberry sauce!

Woman: No. Thanksgiving is people.

TEN FAT TURKEYS

by Jane K. Priewe

This activity for ten youngsters is used for fun, to get rid of the wiggles, or to present to other classes. The activity can be repeated with ten different children, so that everyone who wants to join in will have the opportunity. Each participant is given a number (1 through 10) and is told that when his number is mentioned, he must fit his actions to the reader's words and leave the group.

Ten fat turkeys wandering through the pine
One got lost, then there were nine. *(turkeys walk in a circle, #10 leaves)*

Nine fat turkeys roosting on a gate
One fell off, then there were eight. *(turkeys squat side by side, #9 topples over)*

Eight fat turkeys tried to fly to heaven
One never came down, then there were seven.
(turkeys fly in a circle, #8 flies off)

Seven fat turkeys eating juicy ticks
One coughed and choked, then there were six.
(turkeys walk in a circle bobbing heads, #7 chokes and exits)

Six fat turkeys happy to be alive
One danced and broke a toe, then there were five.
(turkeys dance in a circle, #6 trips and limps away)

Five fat turkeys found an open door
One went inside, then there were four.
(turkeys walk in a circle, #5 pretends to peer inside and enters)

Four fat turkeys at a jamboree
One leaped too high, then there were three.
(turkeys skip and hop in a circle, #4 jumps away)

Three fat turkeys in a birch canoe
One fell overboard, then there were two.
(turkeys sit one behind the other, #3 falls overboard)

Two fat turkeys looking for some fun
Had a race, one couldn't stop, then there was one.
(turkeys trot in a circle, #2 runs away)

One fat turkey after the race he'd won
Went to buy an ice cream cone, then there were none.
(turkey struts off, stage empty)

Ten fat turkeys all have gone away
Let's hope there'll be plenty more for this Thanksgiving Day!
(ten new turkeys take their places as this last verse is read)

THANKSGIVING BASKET

by Evelyn Witter

Time: The day before Thanksgiving.
Characters: SUE, DAVID, CLARA and OTTO.
Scene: Any room in the school. As the scene opens, Sue and David are packing a Thanksgiving basket. Canned goods are on the table.

SUE: *(packing)* I don't think we have enough food.

DAVID: *(working with crepe paper and scissors as he covers basket)* I don't think so either. I can't understand it. The teachers have been reminding everyone for the last three weeks.

SUE: We've had several lessons on the meaning of Thanksgiving, too. It's like our homeroom teacher said: "Sharing food with those in need is one way to show our thankfulness for our blessings and our thoughtfulness of others."

DAVID: If food was hard to get, that would be different. But all we have to do is reach up to the shelf and help ourselves.

SUE: *(pausing)* I guess most of the children figured bringing food was not important or they just plain forgot.

DAVID: *(stopping, too...speaks with feeling)* Not important! Forgot! If you were in a family that didn't have enough food for Thanksgiving you'd think it was important, and you wouldn't be able to forget it, either!

SUE: *(in soothing tones)* Now David, don't get so wrought up! And speaking of forgetting...I wonder if Clara and Otto Lutz forgot we were packing the basket today. They told me last Sunday they would bring groceries by the time they were needed.

DAVID: I wouldn't count on them. They are poor themselves. With their father being sick for so long, I know they don't have much money.

SUE: I know. They even have to go out baby sitting and run errands to get money.

DAVID: And they help the family by working with their mother to raise a garden for their food.

SUE: One thing is sure, they can't reach up to the cupboard shelf like the rest of us. I don't blame them if they don't contribute anything.

DAVID: *(sadly)* I guess with their father sick and being so poor, and having to work so hard...they don't have much to be thankful for.

SUE: You're right. *(then looks around in surprise)* David, is this all the food we have?

DAVID: Yep.

SUE: Why this is only half a Thanksgiving basket!

DAVID: *(peers into basket)* Not much, is it?

SUE: *(wringing her hands)* What are we going to do? The family has already been notified that they are going to get a basket from our class. They are depending on it!

DAVID: We can only give what we have. *(shuffling of feet outside)* Sue, do you hear something coming? *(Enter Clara and Otto, carrying a big shopping bag between them. The bag is heavy with garden food, which may include pumpkin, squash, onions, potatoes.)*

OTTO: *(setting bag on floor and smiling)* Are we late?

SUE: No, just in time. We have packed everything we had.

(Continued on page 38)

AN INDIAN THANKSGIVING

by Elaine M. Ward

Jimmy and his family were new to the West. They had lived in the log cabin that Jimmy's father had built for one year and it had been a hard year with little food and much sickness.

"I'm not sure that we can stand another winter without food," Jimmy's father said one cool November day. "Tomorrow I must leave to go into the woods and hunt food."

Jimmy's mother shivered. She had heard stories about the Indians and she was afraid. "Jimmy and I will be all right, but be careful," she managed to say.

Jimmy's father left early the next morning, and Jimmy helped his mother cut wood and feed the chickens. It was a warm November day and while Jimmy worked, he cast a longing eye toward the river. When his chores were finished, he asked his mother, "May I go to the river to fish?"

"While your father is away, I do not want you to go to the river," Mother replied.

"I'll be all right. There are no Indians around here and we need the fish I could catch," Jimmy pleaded with his mother. "Please!"

Jimmy's mother knew how much he wanted to go fishing.

She knew, too, how much they needed the fish for food. At last she agreed that he could go if he would be very careful.

The river was quiet and the day a good one for fishing, for the fish were biting. Jimmy was thoroughly enjoying himself when he heard the cry.

Jimmy looked up and down the river. He had not seen anyone on the river before, but he had been so busy fishing that it was possible that someone had come up the river without his even knowing it. In the distance he could see an arm reach out of the water in the middle of the river. Jimmy ran to the old boat his father kept tied to a tree on the bank. Pushing the boat into the water, he began to row very fast.

Jimmy could still see the arm waving, but he could not understand the shouts. As he rowed closer, he knew why. The person in the river was an Indian!

Jimmy stopped rowing. He remembered his promise to his mother, and he also knew that he was afraid. He could row away and the Indian would never catch him. But if he rowed away, the Indian would drown, for there was no one but Jimmy there to save him. All of these thoughts went through Jimmy's head as he rowed.

Making his decision, Jimmy reached his hand into the water and caught the wrist of the Indian. He pulled and pulled. The Indian slowly opened his eyes. With his last ounce of energy, the Indian threw his body over the side of the boat, as Jimmy grabbed his legs and pulled him into the boat. The Indian lay in the boat without moving.

With all his effort, Jimmy rowed to shore. He pulled the Indian from the boat and onto the land. He pushed up and down on the Indian's back to get the water out of him, as his father had shown him to do. The Indian gave a low, faint moan. With Jimmy's help he sat up. Soon he was on his feet. Then, giving the sign of friendship, he walked toward the woods.

Jimmy stood watching the woods for a long time, until he remembered his mother and the fish and ran all the way home. He planned to tell his mother about the Indian, but when he arrived home and saw his father there, he was so surprised, he forgot all about the Indian.

"What happened, Dad?" Jimmy asked, seeing his father stretched out on the bed.

"I broke my leg while chasing a deer," his father explained. Jimmy could see the pain and dis-

AN INDIAN THANKSGIVING
(Continued from page 37)

appointment in his father's eyes.

"Look, see the fish I caught!" he said.

"Good for you, son," his father replied.

Jimmy's father's leg mended slowly. The fish did not last long. Soon there was no food again. The next day was Thanksgiving, but Father, Mother and Jimmy knew that it would be no different from any other day.

"We have much for which to be thankful," Mother said. "We have a home and we are all together."

Jimmy was about to add his thanksgiving, when he saw the band of Indians approaching their home. What should he do? Father was in bed. Jimmy ran to bar the door. As he did, he recognized the man on the first horse. It was the Indian he had saved in the river. Jimmy opened the door and the Indian made the sign of peace.

"Brave Eagle, mighty chief of the Cherimees, brings you gifts and many thanks," he said in broken English.

Jimmy could think of noth-ing to say as he saw the dried meat, fish, pumpkins, squash, and corn being carried into his house.

That day Chief Brave Eagle and the Indians showed Jimmy's family how to plant the corn. "With this you will have much food," they explained.

When it was time for the Indians to leave, Chief Brave Eagle took Jimmy's hand and the two men smiled at one another, as they waved good-bye.

"Yes, we have much for which to thank God," said Jimmy's mother, putting her arm around his shoulder, "for home and food and now, friendship."

THANKSGIVING BASKET
(Continued from page 36)

DAVID: We have only half a basket.

CLARA: See, Otto! *(begins unpacking shopping bag and turns to Sue and David)* Otto said he didn't think these things were nice enough to bring because all the others brought fancy canned goods.

DAVID: *(hurries over to help Clara and holds up a sack of onions)* Not nice enough. It all looks good to me!

OTTO: But these are only things we raised in our garden.

SUE: *(raising her eyebrows)* You're willing to share what you worked so hard for all spring and summer and fall? And didn't you plan to store this food for winter?

CLARA: We're thankful we have enough to share!

OTTO: Yes. Thankful for the good earth, the rain, the sun that God gave us so we could raise such a big garden.

SUE: *(helping David and Clara put produce in the basket)* Oh, Clara! Otto! Your garden produce has filled the basket to the very top. We can give a whole Thanksgiving basket now!

OTTO: *(standing back to admire the basket)* A basket like that shows our class is thoughtful and thankful.

SUE: And I think Clara and Otto are the most thoughtful and thankful of us all.

A GUEST FOR THANKSGIVING

by Jane Landreth

"I wonder where this ball came from," the old man leaned down to the ground to pick up the ball. "It must have fallen from the sky."

"Hi, Mr. Greenly," said Bryon peeking from behind the big tree in the yard. Bryon had rolled the ball from around the tree without being seen.

Bryon and Mr. Greenly were accustomed to one another's teasing. They enjoyed playing tricks and games together. Every day Bryon would walk past Mr. Greenly's house and stop and visit with him. Sometimes Bryon would roll the ball from behind the tree. Sometimes he would fly his plane past him. He tried to sneak up on the old man without being seen.

At first Bryon would not speak to the man. He would wave as he passed. His parents had told him to never speak to strangers. But Mr. Greenly would always speak to him.

Bryon told his parents about his new friend who lived down the street. He told them how he waved at him every day and how the old man would talk to him. "Can I talk to him?" he asked. "He doesn't seem to be a stranger to me."

"Yes, you may talk to him," his father answered.

"But don't take any food from him," added Mother.

Usually the only food the man had with him was peanuts and sunflower seeds. He fed them to the squirrels and birds that came into his yard. Mr. Greenly had many trees and bushes in his yard. He even had a bird bath for the birds. He had built many bird feeders. So the animals liked to visit the old man.

Thanksgiving Day came and Bryon was taking a walk down the street while he waited for relatives to come to his house. Bryon thought the man would probably be visiting relatives. He was surprised to see him sitting in his favorite chair watching the birds flutter about in the bird bath.

Bryon darted from tree to tree. "Surprise!" he yelled jumping from behind a big tree. The birds flew into a nearby tree.

Even the old man jumped. "You sure did surprise me today!" he said. "Are you sick? Why aren't you in school at this time of the morning?"

"Don't you know?" asked Bryon. "Today is Thanksgiving!"

"So it is," said the old man. "Guess I forgot."

"My grandma and grandpa are coming for Thanksgiving dinner," said Bryon. "My Uncle Peter, Aunt Marge, and Cousin Jason are coming, too. Mother is cooking a big turkey right now. We're having dressing, cranberry sauce, and pumpkin pie."

"Sounds like you will have quite a feast," said the old man. "I know that you will have a good time today."

"What are you going to do today, Mr. Greenly?" asked Bryon. "Are you going to spend the day with anyone special?"

"Oh, I will spend it with my friends," said Mr. Greenly.

"Good," replied Bryon. "Would you like to play a little catch before I have to go home?"

Mr. Greenly and Bryon tossed the ball back and forth. Soon Bryon looked at his wrist watch. "It's time I was going home," he said. "Mother told me not to stay very long."

"You better hurry," said the old man. "You wouldn't want to be late for all that good food."

"When are your friends coming?" asked Bryon.

"I see some of them coming right now," Mr. Greenly replied pointing toward the sky.

Bryon looked. All he saw was two blue jays swooping down from the big pine tree. There were two squirrels scampering in the trees overhead.

"I mean your friends for

GUEST FOR THANKSGIVING
(Continued from page 39)

Thanksgiving," said Bryon.

"These are my friends. And so are you," said the old man. "And this is Thanksgiving. You and the birds are my Thanksgiving friends. You better hurry and go so your mother won't worry."

"Well, goodbye," said Bryon. "I'll see you tomorrow."

"Happy Thanksgiving," called out Mr. Greenly.

Bryon ran down the street to his house. No cars were in the driveway yet. He was out of breath when he got to the door.

"Where's Grandma and Grandpa?" he asked when he got his breath.

"We won't be having any company," said his mother. "While you were gone Grandpa called. One of the neighbors fell this morning and broke his leg. They can't seem to find any of his relatives. Grandpa feels that they should stay with the neighbor until a relative is located."

"What about Uncle Peter and Aunt Marge?" asked Bryon. "I was looking forward to playing with Cousin Jason."

"They were coming with Grandma and Grandpa," explained Father. "Their car was in the shop getting some work done on it."

"I guess we will have Thanksgiving alone this year," said Mother. "All this food and no one to share it with! We'll be eating turkey for weeks!"

Suddenly Bryon's face lit up. "I know who we could invite for company!"

"But Bryon, this is Thanksgiving Day," said Mother. "People have already made plans for today."

"My friend, Mr. Greenly, hasn't," said Bryon. "He was going to spend this day with the birds and squirrels. Couldn't we ask him?"

"But Bryon, we don't even know this man," said Father.

"But I know him," replied Bryon. "He's my friend."

"You don't understand," said Mother. "He's a stranger to us."

"You are always telling me to share. In church school we talk about ways to share what we have with others," started Bryon. "Why can't we share Thanksgiving dinner with someone who will not have one?"

Bryon's parents looked at each other.

"Well, I guess you have a point, son," said Father. "I'll walk down to your friend's house with you and we'll ask him to come to dinner."

"I'll finish things here," said Mother.

A little later there were four people sitting around the table— Bryon, his mother, his father, and Mr. Greenly. They bowed their heads while Bryon thanked God for the food and friends.

"It's been a long time since I had a feast like this," said the old man with a tear in his eye. "Thanks for inviting me."

"It was Bryon's idea," said Father.

"And we are glad you could come," added Mother. "Bryon sometimes calls you his special friend."

"This will always be a Thanksgiving to remember," said the old man looking at Bryon.

THANKSGIVING

by Jane K. Priewe

T is for "Thank you!" Say it often, and mean it.
H is for happy. You'll know it when you've seen it.
A stands for alert. Watch for when you are needed.
N is for natural. Be yourself and you've succeeded.

K stands for knowledge. This you gain through the years.
S is for strength. Like when one perseveres.
G is for generous. With cash, talent, and time.
I stands for innocent. To be pure is no crime.
V stands for victor. One who strives, gains, and wins.

I is for interest. Knowing where all begins.
N stands for nice. You'll never want for friends.
G is for gentle. Always ready to make amends.
Just a few of these traits make us well-liked and sought.
But it's plainly a fact. Not one trait can be bought.

ACTIVITIES

PARTICIPATING IN THANKSGIVING

by Elaine M. Ward

"In everything give thanks." I Thessalonians 5:18

Giving thanks and showing love is the way we celebrate God's love for us at Thanksgiving. Children express love, joy, and thanksgiving through participation in the act of worship, stories, and activities. Children learn all the time by what they hear and what they see, but especially by what they do. Gratitude is an attitude. It cannot begin too soon.

Thanksgiving is the day we worship the Lord. As the young child said, "This is the day we 'wash up' the Lord!"

A. Let them hear!

1. Stories and books model and help children express their thankfulness. Read a story of your choice.

2. Children enjoy the rhythm and rhyme of poetry:

Dear God, hear and bless
Thy beasts and singing birds:
And guard with tenderness
Small things that have no words.[1]

3. Music allows children to express their feelings in words. Turn off the lights and light a candle. Sit in the silence on the floor in a circle and play "Hide Me"[2] (or a song of your choosing) and read Psalm 17:8: "Keep me as the apple of your eye: hide me in the shadow of your wings."

B. Let them see!

1. View filmstrips, videos, movies, such as "The Thanksgiving Feast" story.[3] Discuss what the children see or hear by asking questions, such as "For what were Turkey, Sweet Potato, Bean, and Pig thankful? What makes you glad? What happens at your house on Thanksgiving? Why do we celebrate Thanksgiving Day?"

2. Pictures. If you have two copies of the story you use, cut one up and ask the children to place the pictures in proper sequence or cut flannel figures for children to place on flannelboard while retelling the story.

3. Picture Cubes. Paste one large picture or a collage of pictures expressing the theme of Thanksgiving on a large square box. Have a variety of magazines or art supplies. Some of the children may prefer to work in groups and some may prefer to write rather than draw or paint on their boxes.

4. Place pictures of life in Palestine when Jesus lived and take a walk, pointing out and discussing what Jesus might have seen. Relate what is seen and discussed to Thanksgiving in Jesus' time.

5. Visit the sanctuary. As you walk and look, ask questions such as "What happens here? Why do we have...What is the meaning of..." (baptismal font, altar, lectern, Bible, cross, Christian flag, etc.) Sit. Sing. Pray. Experience silence in the sanctuary, in the presence of God.

C. Let them do!

1. Write a litany, such as the characters in the story sang, asking each child to name something for which they are thankful and say together the words, "We give thanks to you, O God." (Psalm 75:1)

2. Interview persons on the telephone, asking, "For what are you thankful this Thanksgiving?" or "What was your happiest Thanksgiving?" After simulated play, visit an adult class, prearranged, and have each child interview one adult.

3. Try these activities.

a. Bring offerings of money or food items for needy persons.

b. Play "have" and "have-nots". Divide the children into two groups, the "haves" and the "have-nots" and cut doughnuts into enough pieces to feed the "haves." Open the Bible and read: "Jesus said, 'Feed the hungry, for when you give to the hungry, you are giving to me.'" (Matthew 25:40, paraphrased.) Have doughnuts for the "have-nots" after discussing the words.

c. Make and share turkey apples. Have an apple, toothpicks, raisins, and stuffed olives for each child. The head is the olive, pieces of pimiento for wattle, and raisins on toothpicks as feathers.

d. Create puppets. Cut out or draw pictures of the characters in the story and paste them to glue sticks or tongue depressors for the children to participate in the retelling of the story.

4. Fingerplays encourage group participation and memorization. Demonstrate by holding up one hand with fingers and thumb stretched apart while saying **"Turkey."**[4]

Here is my turkey.
Listen, he will speak.
"These are my feathers, (wiggle fingers)
This is my beak. (wiggle thumb)
Thanksgiving is sharing
And having fun...for you... (point to children)
Not me! (point to self, shake head)
So watch me run!" (hide hand behind back)

All About Thanksgiving[5]

(Have appropriate pictures to hold up or put on a flannelgraph as words are used.)

Come, let's do a fingerplay all about Thanksgiving Day,

Putting pictures on the board that will help us thank the Lord.

God, we thank you for our bread (1), for our home (2) and our warm bed (3),

For food we eat (4), for rain (5), and sun (6), Mother (7), Father (8), everyone (9),

For the flower (10), bird (11), and tree (12), and for friends (13) like you and me!

5. Creative Movement allows children to move and to use their imaginations.

a. Let's pretend we are turkeys. How would we move? Use the fingerplay above. Then move from the joy of the story of Thanksgiving to the joy of worship. Sing a song or hymn of Thanksgiving and read Psalm 100.

b. Use lightweight scarfs in a variety of colors, lengths and shapes for the children to hold and move to create designs in the air while listening and moving to chosen music. You might attach the scarves to long sticks and move them to a reading of the Psalm above. Encourage them to create and feel for themselves.

6. Dramatic Play provides opportunities for acting out stories.

a. Act out the story "The Thanksgiving Feast."

b. Read John 13:1-20 of how Jesus washed his disciples' feet as a sign of service and thanksgiving. Tell the story from scripture and let the children play it. Use it as a springboard for talking about ways to serve because we are thankful for all that we have and because we love God.

7. Creative Art is a meaningful way for children to express their thanks and love.

a. Make a Thanksgiving Mural. On a long sheet of paper write in large letters words of thanks from the Bible, such as, "We give thanks to you, O God (Ps. 75:1) or Give thanks to the Lord" for cutting, placing, and pasting, or art media for expressions of thanks, such as tempera paint, felt-tipped markers or crayons. Discuss the representations of thanksgiving as children work.

b. Make Thanksgiving plaques as gifts from tree bark, kernels of corn, yarn, and glue. The children will glue the kernels on the bark in a design. Glue on yarn to hang.

c. Make Thanksgiving wall hangings. Use an old toothbrush, screen, shoe box, white shoe polish or tempera paint, leaves, straight pins, paper, cloth, aprons, newspapers, paste, and strips of paper with the Bible verse "We give thanks to thee, O God."

Cover the working area with newspapers and children with aprons. Pin the leaves in a design on cloth. Set the screen on open shoe box. Rub the brush in white coloring and over the screen until the desired area is spattered. Paste the verse below the leaves.

d. Make Thanksgiving Place Mats: cut muslin with pinking shears into pieces 11" x 16" and draw a picture or design with wax crayons. Place a piece of brown wrapping paper over the drawing and press with a warm iron to make it permanent.

8. Prayer and Worship are the high points of this day. Make prayer booklets children can use in and outside of class.

Ask them to copy the words and create designs or pictures to illustrate them. The words are those of Richard of Chichester:

Day by day,
Dear Lord, of Thee three things I pray:
To see Thee more clearly,
Love Thee more dearly,
Follow Thee more nearly,
Day by Day.

So we say...and pray...participating on Thanksgiving Day.

[1]**Unknown, Poems and Prayers For the Very Young,** Martha Alexander, Random House, N.Y., 1973.

[2]**Dandelions,** Mary Lu Walker, Paulist Press, N.Y., 1975.

[3]"The Thanksgiving Feast," **The Story Tree** filmstrip or video, Tabor Publications, Allen, Texas, 1981.

[4]**Be and Say a Fingerplay,** Elaine M. Ward, Educational Ministries, Brea, CA, 1981.

[5]Ibid.

DISCUSSION STARTERS

WHAT IF...

If you could invite someone special that you admire a great deal for Thanksgiving dinner (someone outside of your family), whom would you ask to come?

If you could invite someone from the past (not living), who might that be? Why did you select that person? What qualities do you admire about him/her? What questions would you ask him/her during dinner? What could you learn from this person?

THANKS!

If you had to list ten people that you are thankful for and rank them in order of their importance, who would they be? How would you express your thankfulness for each of the ten people you listed? Would it be difficult to express thankfulness to some of the people? Why? If you had to plan a service of "thankfulness" what would you include in the service and why?

THANKS FOR WHAT?

When we think of Thanksgiving we may visualize many different things. Perhaps we might think of the Pilgrims and the first Thanksgiving where the Indians and Pilgrims shared food together about a common table. We might also think of the religious freedom the Pilgrims were searching for in a new land. Others might think of the harvest and the meaning of having such variety and quality of food to eat. The list can go on and on, but today as you think of Thanksgiving, what do you think of? What are you thankful for this year?

On a piece of paper list eight things for which you are thankful at this time. (Some suggestions might be: school, family, church, friends, being helpful to others, being loving and being loved, etc.)

After you have made your list, go back and place a number in front of each item and rank them from 1-8 (most important to least important). What are you must thankful for?

DISCUSSION STARTERS

THE PILGRIM'S WORLD

Have a discussion with your class about what it was like here when the pilgrims landed. Stress the environmental aspects: clean air, fertile soil, wild animals, virgin forests, etc. Then discuss how we have treated our land since the pilgrim's arrival. Are we taking good care of God's beautiful world? How can we improve our environment? Are we thankful for what we have in our land this Thanksgiving? What is one thing that each of us can do to make this a better land?

IF I WERE A PILGRIM CHILD

As Thanksgiving approaches and you begin discussing the Pilgrims, set aside some class time for story writing. After some background discussion about the Pilgrims and their time, ask the youngsters to write a story entitled "If I Were a Pilgrim Child..." depicting what the child's life was like and why the Pilgrims came here. If the stories turn out well, have the children record their stories on tape and share them with younger classes in the church school.

INDIANS

At this time of year we talk a lot about the Pilgrims and how the Indians helped them, but what do we know about native American Indians today? Make it a class project to gain some current information about them.

1. Does your local church have any connections to the Indians? Are there local agencies for the Indians? Does your denomination have any national programs for Indians? Does your Outreach Committee (Social Concerns Mission or whatever) have any priority about dealing with Indian concerns?

2. Did any native Indian tribes ever inhabit your area? Do any Indians live in your community today? Where do they work? How do they support themselves? What are their concerns today? How can we help them?

3. How are Indians presented in the local school curriculum? Do the youngsters in your class have stereotypes about them? What can we do about that?

4. What do our children learn about Indians from T.V.? Write your local T.V. station with your concerns.

5. Write to some Native-American Organizations for current information about their concerns:

a. American Indian Historical Society
   1451 Masonic Ave.
   San Francisco, CA 94117

b. Americans for Indian Opportunity
   1816 Jefferson Place, N.W.
   Washington, DC 20036

c. Association on American
   Indian Affairs, Inc.
   432 Park Ave. So.
   New York, NY 10016

d. Indian Rights Association
   1505 Race St.
   Philadelphia, PA 19102

I AM THANKFUL FOR...

by Jane Landreth

In Autumn the trees are covered with red, orange, yellow, green, and brown leaves. Red apples are being picked from the trees. Corn stalks with big round orange pumpkins hidden in them can be found in fall gardens.

We can decorate this learning center with all the items from this beautiful season. Use leaves of various colors, pumpkins, corn stalks, turkeys, and apples to decorate the four sections of the learning center: Falling Leaves, Basket of Apples, Pumpkins and Cornstalks, and Turkeys.

Stories that can be used in this learning center are: God Made the Earth, Genesis 1; God Takes Care of Noah, Genesis 6-8; God Cared on a Long Trip, Exodus 15:22-26, 16:1-15; Worshiping God, Nehemiah 8-9; Two Good Friends, 1 Samuel 18-20; The Good News, Luke 24:1-35.

Memory verses could include: Psalm 95:2, Psalm 107:1, Psalm 9:1, James 1:17, 1 Peter 5:7.

Falling Leaves

Decorate this area with different colored leaves. Make a title strip. Let the children choose from two projects.

The Thankful Tree. Place a small branch in a pot filled with dirt. Cut colored leaves and lay them under the tree. The children can write something for which they are thankful on the leaves and attach them to the tree.

Walking Through the Leaves. Make a gameboard. Draw leaves with small footprints on a posterboard. Make small cards with numbers to five. Use buttons for each child who wants to play the game.

To play, start at "God." Draw a number. Advance that many footprints. If the footprint tells you to do something, do it. If you cannot do what the footprint says, go back two steps. Suggestions for the footprints are:

Questions from any of the Bible stories.
Name someone you are thankful for.
Who is your very best Friend?
How can we worship God?
Name something for which you are thankful.
The winner is the child who advances to "Stop" first.

Basket of Apples

Decorate this area with a basket filled with construction paper apples. Make a title strip and attach to the basket. On the apples print "Who Am I" questions. Suggestions for the apples are:

I made all things on the earth and in the heavens. Who am I? (Genesis 1:1)
I built a big boat and took the animals into it. Who am I? (Genesis 6:13-14)
I prayed to God for water and manna from heaven to take care of the children of Israel. Who am I? (Exodus 15:22)
I gave David my robe to show my love for him. Who am I? (1 Samuel 18:3,4)
I read the book of the law of God to the people. Who am I? (Nehemiah 8:5)
I went to the tomb looking for Jesus. Who am I? (Luke 24:10)

Make other questions from the Bible stories that are used.

Pumpkins and Cornstalks

Decorate this area with pumpkins and cornstalks. Make a title strip. Let the children choose one of the two projects.

String Pumpkins. Cut several pumpkins from construction paper. Draw things for which you are thankful on the pumpkins. Punch holes at the top of the pumpkins. String them together with yarn. Use for a room decoration.

Choose a Cornstalk. Place half squares of paper on each cornstalk. On each of the squares of paper, print an activity for the childen to do. Activity ideas might include:

Read Psalm 100. Write a sentence telling about the Psalm.
Read Psalm 23. Write a sentence telling about the Psalm.
Draw a picture showing a way God takes care of us.
Choose a memory verse and learn it.
Write a Thank You poem.
Choose a memory verse to illustrate.

Turkeys

Decorate the area of the room with turkeys. Make a title strip. Let the boys and girls choose from two projects.

Make a Bible Marker. Make a Bible marker in the shape of a turkey. Print one of the memory verses on the marker. Give it to a friend.

Thanksgiving Card. Cut two turkey shapes from construction paper. Staple the sides together to make a card. Decorate the front of the card. Print a message or Bible verse inside the card. Give to a friend or someone who is sick or lonely.

A TURKEY FINGER PLAY

by Jane K. Priewe

Can you make a turkey
With a wattle, long and red? *(Wiggle fingers under chin)*
And can you make him strut and prance *(Strut/prance in place)*
While he bobs his round, brown head? *(Bob head)*
He spreads his tail in a feathery fan. *(With stiff arms, bring hands up from sides to meet overhead)*
He looks for food on the way. *(Look from side to side)*
So that he'll be big and fat *(Arms held out in a circle in front of body)*
For Thanksgiving Day! *(Bow head and hold hands to pray)*

TEACHING THANKFULNESS TO PRIMARY CHILDREN

by Evelyn Witter

Thankfulness is not a theme to be used only at the Thanksgiving season. Thankfulness should be impressed on primary children at every opportunity. All seasons are suitable to remind children of the beauty or bounty of God's wonderful world and to inspire thankfulness in their hearts for their many blessings.

One very effective way to accomplish this aim is through the use of handicraft materials, purposefully designed to make the children work at and think through what thankfulness means to them. This is how it was done in one Primary Department.

First of all the materials were assembled, such as:

1. Various color shades of manila paper suitable for the particular season.
2. Silhouettes of girls and boys cut from black paper (hands shown folded in prayer.)
3. Gummed pictures of flower or fruits.
4. Gummed pictures of an open Bible.

The manila paper was cut into rectangles, 8 x 6 inches. These were folded 2 inches in from each 6-inch end to make 2 closing flaps that met in the center, thus making a folder. This was cut in a curve at one 4-inch end to simulate the Gothic curve of a church window.

In the middle section of the opened folder, the teachers printed: "A Thank You to God." At the bottom of the middle section they printed: "It is a good thing to give thanks." (Psalm 92:1).

On each flap, about 2 inches from the curved top was printed: "For."

In class, after the children were seated at their work tables, the folders were distributed, and each child selected a silhouette according to whether a boy or a girl.

"This is supposed to be a picture of you giving thanks to God," the teacher told them. "The Bible tells us, 'It is a good thing to give thanks.' And since we find this verse in the Bible, I want you to paste a little Bible right after the words, and write Psalm 92:1 under it. This tells where in the Bible we can find this verse."

Then the stickers of various flowers or fruits were laid out on the table.

"God has made our world a delightful place. Flowers and fruit are part of that delight. Pick out two of the flowers or fruits you are most thankful for, and paste them in the upper corners of each flap.

"We are happy to give thanks, aren't we? In Psalm 100 we read, 'Come before his presence with singing.' Let's use a little, golden harp to remind us of this, and draw it at the very top in the center.

"Now, on each inside flap of your thankfulness folder there is room for you to write down all the things you are thankful for. Write down as many as you can think of."

The lists grew quickly. An interesting variety of items appeared on the folders. The project was successful. Through doing, hearing, seeing, and feeling the children had grasped something of the meaning of thankfulness.

THANKSGIVING, THE OLD TESTAMENT WAY

by Jane Landreth

How would you like to eat your Thanksgiving meal outdoors in the shelter of green branches and fruit with the sun shining? Sound like fun? Many Jewish boys and girls eat their meal this way. It is called the Feast of Booths rather than Thanksgiving. It happens about the same time as we have our Thanksgiving, in the autumn of the year. It is a time of celebration and feasting and praising God. It began in the Old Testament times.

In autumn when the crops of figs, grapes, olives, and grain were harvested, the Hebrew people celebrated the Feast of Booths for seven days. Each family built the booth on the roof top or in the court-yard of the homes. Many families together might build a booth in the temple or on the city square. The booth was an open framework made of slats with green branches woven into the frame. The children of the families decorated the inside with fruit and flowers.

The holiday usually occurred in October. Instructions for conducting the feast were given by God in Leviticus 23:39-40. No one was to go hungry. If someone was in need of food, the others were required to share theirs.

The Hebrew families lived in these booths to remind them of the days God took care of their people when they lived in tents in the wilderness. At the feast each family thanked God for the good harvest that they had been given.

Today Jewish families still celebrate the Feast of Booths. Sometimes booths are built on balconies of apartments or in the backyards of homes. Some-times booths are built in living areas of homes. Sometimes the booths are built in the yard of a Hebrew school or a synagogue so that everyone in the community can feast together.

In the hot, dry Bible times, people did not have to worry about the weather. Today in the colder countries, the weather affects the celebration.

Today in the lands where there is freedom to worship, the preparation for the Feast of Booths is a joyous project.

In the United States in November we celebrate Thanksgiving Day, which is a little like the Feast of Booths. The pumpkin, squash, turkey, and ears of corn are symbols of the American harvest festival. The pilgrims set aside the first Thanksgiving day to give thanks for God's bountiful blessings.

The children will have a good time building their own Feast of Booths. Secure a large box in which an appliance has been packed. Provide tempera paints or brown wrapping paper to cover the box. Use green construction paper or painted newspapers cut into strips to cover the roof (long branches could be used).

Let the children develop the ideas as to how the booth should look. They may read in Leviticus 23:33-44 for help in gaining ideas.

After the Feast of Booths has been built, the children might like to decorate the inside with vegetables and fruits. If fresh fruits and vegetables are not available, the children can paint them on the inside walls of the booth.

Planning an order of worship can also be fun. Make a scroll with the words from Leviticus 23:33-44 on it. Let a child read the passage of scripture. Sing some praise songs that the children know. Have a time of prayer thanking God for all the blessings that He gives us. Read some Bible verses of praise— Psalm 92:1, Psalm 119:16, Psalm 147:1, Psalm 33:5, and Psalm 107:1.

The children might want to act out the time of feasting and thanksgiving. They may dress as Old Testament characters. Have available large pieces of fabric, scarfs, ties, towels, and robes.

Make this a fun time along with a learning experience that the children will talk about even in later years as they look back to Thanksgiving memories.

SERVICE PROJECT

by Linda Davidson

Here is a project in which to involve your high school youth group that will be fun and also worthwhile at the same time. Weeks before Thanksgiving advertise in your church newsletter and/or bulletin that the youth group will be packaging fruit baskets for shut-ins the Sunday before Thanksgiving. Ask church members for contributions of fresh fruit, unshelled nuts, dried fruit, wrapped candy and small wicker baskets. Set up an attractive table where people can deposit their contributions on the stated Sunday.

Get a list from your minister of shut-ins or those who would enjoy receiving a fruit basket. The Sunday afternoon following the fruit collection, have the youth group meet to make up the fruit baskets. You will need to have on hand: large disposable plastic plates (in case you don't have enough baskets), plastic wrap or colored cellophane, ribbon and gift enclosure cards. Divide the fruit among the number of baskets you are making. Arrange it attractively and fill in spaces with nuts and candy. If you have access to Easter grass, it makes a nice bed for the fruit. Wrap the plates or baskets with plastic wrap and tie with a ribbon. If you are doing quite a number of these, set up an assembly line. While those are being put together, have someone address the gift enclosure cards and then attach one securely to each basket.

When the baskets are done, divide the youth in teams, with one driver for each group. Distribute the fruit baskets among the teams, and send them on their way. (Divide groups into geographical areas so each team is not criss-crossing the town.) The minister may want to send along bulletins or tapes of sermons or some other publicity or greetings to these folks. The young people are to deliver the baskets and spend a few minutes with each recipient.

THANKSGIVING ACROSS THE MILES

by Jane Landreth

Thanksgiving is traditionally a holiday when family members gather together and eat turkey, cranberries, and pumpkin pie. But many times some of the relatives cannot be there. Unlike earlier years, families are moving from place to place now. This sometimes makes it impossible for all the relatives to be together on Thanksgiving. What can be done about those relatives that are unable to attend the Thanksgiving festivities?

Send a Thanksgiving card across the miles. Let the children make a card. Show them how to fold a sheet of paper. Let them decorate the outside cover. The inside can be a poem, a saying, a verse, or a note. The children might wish to say: "I'm thanking God for the best grandmother in the world." "Wish you were here to spend Thanksgiving with us." "God loves you and so do I. Happy Thanksgiving." Be sure to send the card in time for it to reach the person across the miles before Thanksgiving.

A Thanksgiving letter telling all the recent happening in the family would make an interesting gift to a relative who has not been in contact with the family in a while. Sending a recent photo is a good idea.

A Thanksgiving tape is an interesting idea. Make the tape before Thanksgiving and make sure it gets across the miles before that special day. Let each member of the family say a few words. Perhaps a song can be sung, a poem can be said, a riddle told. Make the tape a fun event.

Making the tape on Thanksgiving Day would let the relatives far away know what kind of a Thanksgiving that they missed. Perhaps a play could be written for the family to tape. Tell what food was being eaten on that special day. The family might give a "talk show." Make the tape special. Mail the tape in a padded envelope.

Remember to watch for ideas throughout the year. This new Thanksgiving tradition of reaching those we love across the miles just might become a hit!

A FAMILY ACTIVITY

by Jane K. Priewe

Here's a family activity for Thanksgiving Day which could turn into a yearly project. It could also make a much-cherished gift for a family, friend, or relative.

To begin, make a small notebook, 7" x 5". The cover can be as fancy or as plain as you choose to make it. Brightly colored construction paper makes a good starting point to hold loose leaf or typing paper cut to size. Be sure to have enough pages, so that every family member or friend in the Thanksgiving Day group has two pages in the book.

If you don't have one of your own, someone might lend you a Polaroid camera. On Thanksgiving Day as guests arrive, take a solo picture of each person. Paste a Polaroid picture on a page, saving the opposite page for another purpose. Once all the pictures are in the booklet, ask everyone to write something on the page opposite his or her picture. What they write doesn't have to be deep or philosophical, but encourage people to write something about this day or another Thanksgiving Day or about some thought or a pleasant memory.

Once the booklet is completed, share the pictures and what's been written. Take a group shot for the cover. If there is a family shut-in who was unable to attend, this little book makes a lovely gift. You can also pack the book away until next year to reread or remind you and your family of last year's Thanksgiving Day.

OUR FIRST THANKSGIVING

Directions: Circle the words which are printed forward, backward, up, down and diagonally.

AMERICA	MAYFLOWER
AX	MEETING
BABY	PILGRIMS
BENCH	PLOW
BRADFORD	PLYMOUTH
BREWSTER	POTS
CABIN	PRAY
CHILD	ROCK
CORN	SCOUT
DEER	STORMS
FRIENDS	TASK
GOD	TEACH
GUN	THANKSGIVING
HARDSHIP	TURKEY
HOUSE	WILD
INDIANS	WIRE
LAND	WOOD
LOVE	WORK

```
T U O C S Y S D N E I R F D
U H M O R A X N S H E V O L
R D A R O R M A S T O R A I
K R Y N C P P L Y M O U T H
E O F U K D I L G B R P S C
Y F L G L S L H O H A O A E
K D O I D O G P S W C B T K
R A W O O D R I N D I A N S
O R E E D X I F V N R R E A
W B R S Q A M E R I C A E T
N L B R E W S T E R N C H Y
B E N C H M E E T I N G T B
```

MURAL MESSAGES

by Phyllis Vos Wezeman

Thanksgiving is a time of the year when people pause to ponder their many blessings. During this season, as well as throughout the year, it is especially appropriate to remember people in the local community, nation and world who do not have adequate food or material goods. Reflect particularly on hunger and its myths and causes, but also spend time seeking and stressing solutions to the issue.

A mural can be an effective way to enable people to work together to explore this theme. After all, it will only be through the cooperation of all that problems can be turned into possibilities.

Materials:
Roll of white shelf paper
Markers or crayons
Tape
Index cards

Procedure: On index cards, write suggested ways in which people can help to prevent hunger. Write a separate idea on each card. If the ideas are in a particular sequence, number the cards in that order. The number of cards necessary will depend on the size of the group and the amount of time available for the activity.

Suggestions to write on the cards will vary with the age of the participants. Sample themes for older children or adults may include:

- Attend discussion groups about hunger.
- Read Christian newsletters, books and magazines that deal with hunger.
- Organize a workshop on the topic.
- Express concern by writing letters.
- Contact local, state and national representatives when hunger issues are being addressed.
- Support world hunger organizations.

- Support community programs such as soup kitchens and food banks.
- Evaluate diet, food budget, food waste and energy consumption.
- Work for economic justice.
- Plan or participate in a fund raising event, such as a soup supper, from which the money can be donated to a hunger relief organization.

Spread the roll of paper on a work space such as a long table or on the floor. Place markers at appropriate intervals.

Explain to the group that they will be working cooperatively to make a mural depicting ways in which people can help to alleviate hunger. Instruct them to work individually or divide them into teams. Allow each person or team to develop their own idea for the mural, or distribute the suggestion cards which have been prepared in advance. Direct participants to use the markers to illustrate the idea or suggestion on the appropriate part of the paper.

Tape the completed mural to the wall and discuss the ideas presented on it.

Note: The action suggestions are based on material from Church World Service, a relief and development organization which works in ninety countries of the world. Additional literature on the myths and causes of hunger may be obtained by writing the main office at P.O. Box 968, Elkhart, Indiana 46515.

TURKEY TABLE FAVORS

Here are some simple turkey table favors that children can make for the family celebration from simple household items. For each one, the wattle and tail feathers are made the same, although you can vary their size, depending on what is used for the body.

Make wattle and tail feathers from construction paper. Fringe tail feathers if desired. The head and wattle are cut all in one piece. If you want extra strength for this piece, use a double thickness of paper. Then fold tabs back at bottom of neck and glue in place on the favor.

NUT CUP FAVORS: Glue wattle and tail feathers to a paper nut cup. Add nuts or candy!

FRUIT OR VEGETABLE FAVOR: Make a turkey favor from a lemon, orange or potato. Push golf tees into the bottom of the body for support. Glue tail feathers to toothpicks and insert into body. Attach wattle with straight pins.

WATTLE AND TAIL

FRINGE EDGES

CUT 5 OR 6

CUT TWO →

FOLD

SPOOL FAVOR: Glue a half of a golf tee to an empty spool of thread, making a base. Add the wattle and tail feathers.

YARN FAVOR: Wrap yarn into a small ball. Glue a bottle cap to the underside of the yarn ball. Add wattle and tail.

WALNUT FAVOR: Glue a wattle and tail to a walnut. Then glue walnut to a plastic bottle cap for the base.

TURKEYS

Here are two ways to make interesting turkeys. For a Yarn Print Turkey, you will need: yarn, glue, cardboard, tempera paint or ink, and paper. Outline a turkey with yarn on a piece of cardboard. Glue down and let dry completely. Then brush the outline with the tempera or ink and print onto a piece of paper. Use these for the front of Thanksgiving cards.

For a Kernel Turkey, glue down a black yarn outline on cardboard of a turkey (front view with feathers showing all around body). Then glue on all colors and sizes of beans and/or kernels of Indian corn in the various sections of the outline.

THANKFUL

by Linda S. Davidson

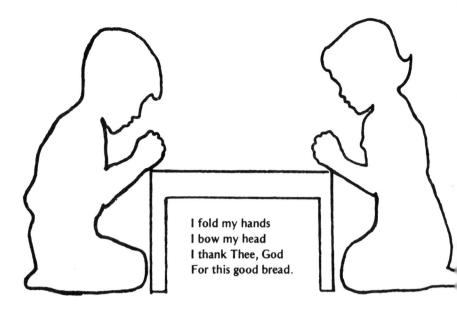

I fold my hands
I bow my head
I thank Thee, God
For this good bread.

You will need: construction paper, patterns for three pieces shown in the illustration (table and 2 children praying), scissors, pencil, and glue.

Here is a simple project children can do at home or church school. Have them trace each of the three pieces shown in the illustration here. Exact cutting is not necessary — just a broad general outline of two children praying is all that is needed. Or they can just draw a picture of two children praying at a table. Next glue the three pieces to a large piece of construction paper. Print the following prayer:

I fold my hands
I bow my head
I thank Thee, God
For this good bread.

When they are done, discuss what "thankful" means and why we pray to God. Repeat the prayer several times so they can say it for their family's Thanksgiving dinner or for any meal.

FOOTPRINT TURKEY

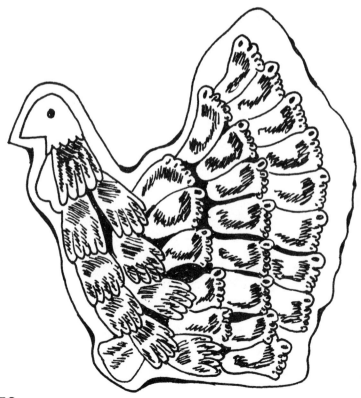

Here's a fun turkey to make for a bulletin board, but it will be messy so plan carefully! Fill aluminum pie pans with several fall-colored tempera paints. Have each child remove his/her right sock and shoe. Step into the paint and then onto a sheet of contrasting-colored paper. Each child will probably be able to get two prints from one dip! Have the children wash and dry their feet immediately! Then repeat the process with one hand. After the prints are dry, have the children cut loosely around them.

Draw a large turkey from a piece of poster board. Tack him to the bulletin board. Add footprint "feathers", starting on the outside with the largest ones and working to the inside with smaller ones and the hand prints. You may want to add some blank shapes for contrasting color and to fill odd corners. Add the head, wattle and feet from construction paper.

FRUIT FROM BALLOONS

by Linda S. Davidson

You will need: small balloons, yarn or string, Plaster of Paris, paint, pipe cleaners, crepe paper, basket or cornucopia.

Try this clever way to make fruit for a cornucopia this year. If your church has an all-church Thanksgiving Dinner, your class could make these for table decorations and then take them home.

Inflate some balloons. Decide which ones most resemble fruit. Select one and wrap it with yarn or string. Uneven fruit, such as a pear, can be emphasized by wrapping string tighter in one area than another. Next dip the string-wrapped balloon in a creamy mixture of Plaster of Paris. Be sure to work the plaster thoroughly into the string. Let dry. Paint with tempera paints. Add pipe cleaners for stems and crepe paper for leaves.

If you can't locate Plaster of Paris, try doing papier mache. Dip strips of newspaper into a glue mixture (1/2 water and 1/2 glue) and wrap them around the balloons. Put on many layers. When completely dry, then paint them.

For a table decoration, have the fruit spilling from a basket or try making papier mache cornucopias.

THANKSGIVING PLACEMATS

by Linda S. Davidson

For this project you will need: old grocery bags or construction paper, crayons, scissors.

Instead of making Pilgrims or Indians for the Thanksgiving Dinner table this year, try making placemats for everyone who will be there. Cut large rectangles from old grocery bags or use 12 x 18" construction paper and fringe all the way around the edge. Then decorate a placemat for each person who will be at your Thanksgiving Dinner. Think about the person's personality and draw a picture of him/her or something appropriate about the person (like a hobby or interest). Use construction paper cutouts, crayons, stickers, or whatever materials you can find.

Your placemats will be a big hit at Thanksgiving Dinner and everyone, no matter what their age, will appreciate your thoughtfulness.

FOR THE BIRDS

When the weather starts getting colder, remind the children that the birds still need food to survive and we can help them in several ways. They are part of God's world and we can be thankful for them at this time of year.

1. String cranberries and lay them on bushes outside the window. Then the class can watch the birds feed and maybe learn something about animal behavior!

2. To make bacon balls you will need: a nylon mesh bag (like onions come in), cornmeal, birdseed, bacon grease, sand. Make a bacon ball by adding cornmeal and birdseed to room temperature bacon grease. Mix until it is a doughy consistency. Sand or fine gravel can be added for grit. Put the bacon ball in the mesh bag. Tie it shut. Hang it in a tree and the birds can perch on the netting.

3. For a birdfeeder that won't need filling very often, use a coffee can and pie tin, as seen in the illustration. Punch holes in the coffee can with a bottle opener. With wire, connect the pie tin to the coffee can and make a loop at the top to hang it in a tree. Fill with birdseed or sunflower seeds.

4. Peanut butter and birdseed are common ingredients for birdfeeders. Put the mixture in an empty orange or grapefruit half. Hang with yarn. Or roll a pinecone in this mixture and then hang it from a limb. Or try making cornmeal cakes by adding one part peanut butter, two parts birdseed and five parts cornmeal to each part of melted beef suet you use. Spoon into paper-lined muffin tins and cool in the refrigerator. When hardened, the cakes can be removed from the tins. (You can freeze these for later use.) Serve them to the birds in mesh bags or tree cavities or crumble them into an open pie tin.

5. Some fresh fruit hung in a plastic cup or grapefruit half is another simple feeder. Cube some apples and oranges, and add some cranberries. Hang it with string or yarn from a tree branch. Or try a fruit kabob for birds! On a heavy cord, string apple or orange slices, suet, cranberries, unshelled peanuts, old bread or doughnuts, and dates. Hang it in a tree and watch the birds come to feed. See how many kinds of birds you can identify.

BULLETIN BOARD

Here is a quick and easy bulletin board that everyone in the class can contribute to. All you need is one set of large letters which spell "Thanksgiving." Pin the letters vertically down the left side of the bulletin board area. Then pass out squares of paper to each child and have everyone draw something for which they are thankful that begins with a letter in the word "Thanksgiving." Have a discussion first about our many blessings and then give them some time to think about being thankful before letting them start. When their pictures are complete, have each child pin his/her picture across from the appropriate letter on the bulletin board.

A CRAFT OF THANKFULNESS

by Jean Rasmussen

A Thanksgiving turkey craft with the verse, "Giving thanks to the Father," Col. 1:12 NIV, can help you show gratitude, to the Lord, this holiday season.

MATERIALS:

white poster board 8" x 8"
black paper 9" x 9"
brown felt 6" x 9"
red felt 2" x 3"
yellow felt 2" x 3"
2b pencil
scissors
large punch
glue
3" x 5" index card
black marker
ruler

"GIVING THANKS TO THE FATHER."
COL. 1:12 NIV

(Enlarge illustration to 9" x 9")

PROCEDURE:

Cut the white poster board to measure 8" x 8" and 9" x 9" for the black paper frame. Glue the poster board to the paper.

Turn all patterns on the reverse side, so the lines won't show. Using the 2b pencil, trace the four turkey patterns on brown felt. Cut them out and place the pieces on the poster board as shown.

Trace the turkey head on red felt. Cut out the head. Punch out an eye and place the head on the turkey body.

Trace the turkey feet on yellow felt. Cut them out too and place them under the turkey body. Then glue all the pieces.

Using the ruler, index card and black marker, print or type the verse, "Giving thanks to the Father," Col. 1:12 on the card. Outline it with the ruler and black marker before cutting it out to glue on the lower part of the turkey.

Put the turkey on a bulletin board or place it on the mantle where all can see it. Your art can be a graphic way of thanking the Lord this Thanksgiving.

A THANKSGIVING NATURE DISPLAY

by Jane Landreth

Make a Thanksgiving nature display in your church school classroom. Let the boys and girls help make the display. Encourage them to bring nature items that they find in the autumn season.

Start with an 8 inch styrofoam ring. Gather up small nature items such as colorful fallen leaves, nuts, acorns, small pine cones, pumpkin seeds, dried flowers, dry seed pods, carrot tops. Let the children arrange the items on the ring and glue with white glue. Stand the ring up on a table. Arrange fall vegetables such as squash, pumpkins, corn, apples, Indian corn, and ornamental gourds around the ring.

Let one child print Psalm 24:1 on a folded strip of posterboard. Stand the strip beside the arrangement.

THANKSGIVING SCROLL

by Jane Landreth

Materials needed: brown paper sack or paper that looks like parchment paper, gold ribbon, felt-tip markers, scissors.

Cut the paper sack so that it lays flat on the table. Take the scissors and cut off the bottom section. If there is any writing on the sack, you may want to paint over the writing with brown paint. Tear the bottom and the top edges of the sack to make it look rough and uneven.

Look up some Bible verses in the Bible that tells about being thankful or praising God. Some good verses to use are: Psalm 24:1, Psalm 107:1, Psalm 103:2, Psalm 126:3, Psalm 145:21, James 1:17. Choose one of the verses and print it neatly on the brown paper.

Roll both ends of the paper toward the center. Tie with a gold ribbon. Share the scroll and the Bible verse with a friend.

VEGETABLE TURKEY

by Jane Landreth

Turkey centerpieces can be made from various types of vegetables: potato, squash, sweet potato.

Cut a large fan tail from light cardboard. Color or paint feathers on the fantail. Cut a slit in the back of the vegetable used.

Slide the tail in place. Cut a head and neck from cardboard. Color or paint features. Leave tabs on the head and neck sections to insert into the vegetable. Make slits into the vegetable front for the head and neck. Insert pieces. Cut two wings for the turkey. Color or paint. Leave tabs and insert into the vegetable slits on the side.

A stand can be made from a two-inch empty paper towel roll. Paint the stand a bright color. Stand the turkey on the towel roll. Place as a centerpiece.

A THANKSGIVING GRAFFITI

by Jane Landreth

A graffiti is a collection of words, pictures, sketches, and notes that represent thoughts or "mind pictures." Make one at home this Thanksgiving for the family and friends.

You will need a large sheet of paper. Choose a wall or area in a room to place the graffiti. Read Psalm 95:1-6 and Psalm 107:1 yourself and to your family.

Everyday think of things that you can be thankful for. Think of the blessings God has given your family. Use words, poems, pictures, or Bible verses to represent these thankful thoughts. Even little sister or brother can draw something they are thankful for. A colorful boarder can be put around the banner.

Thanksgiving Day can be a sharing day. The family can gather around the banner. Let each family member share what he or she put on the graffiti. Hold hands and say a special prayer thanking God for the family and the special blessings that He gives us each day.

THE THANKS-GIVING BOARD

by Jane Landreth

Thanksgiving is a time for being thankful. We think of all the material things that God has given us—the food, clothing house, family. Thanksgiving is a good time to think of all the people for whom we are thankful. Preparing a Thanks-Giving Board is a project for the children in the church school class.

If there is a bulletin board in the church foyer, ask permission for the use of it during the month of November. If there is no bulletin board available, ask permission to attach a large strip of paper or posterboard to the hallway wall. Print across the top of the board or cut letters out of construction paper the title, "The Thanks-Giving Board."

Ask the children to think of people who have helped them in the church. Ask them to think of people for whom they are thankful. Let the children write thank you notes on small pieces of paper and tack them to the board. They may write: "Thank you, Mrs. Johnson, for helping me learn a memory verse." "Thank you, Mrs. Wilson, for telling me the Bible story about Jesus." "Thank you, Mr. Jones, for giving me a ride home from church." The children will enjoy thinking of the people who have done kind deeds for them. They might remember to thank the people who work at church. "Thank you, Mr. Gilbert, for keeping the church clean." "Thank you, Rev. Brown, for the good sermons you preach to us."

For those who walk by and want to add a thank you note themselves, attach a pad with a pencil to the bulletin board. Attach the pad with thumb tacks or tape. Wrap yarn around the tip of a pencil and attach to the board with a thumb tack. Put a small square sign above the pad and pencil that says, "Do you want to thank someone?"

Announce in church what the bulletin board is being used for. Tell the congregation to share the thanksgiving spirit by saying thanks to people who have been especially kind and helpful. It will be fun for everyone to read the nice things people have to say about them.

PILGRIMS

by Linda Davidson

For this project you will need: styrofoam cups (8 oz.), black paint, nut cups, black and white construction paper, 2-inch styrofoam balls, sequins, pins.

Paint the outside of the styrofoam cup with black paint. (You can cover it with black construction paper instead if desired.) Let dry. Glue the nut cup on the bottom of the styrofoam cup, turned upside down. The nut cup is the neck and the black cup is the body of the pilgrim. If you cannot find white nut cups, cover the colored nut cup with a strip of white paper. Glue the styrofoam ball on for the head. Sequins and pins can be added for facial features.

To make the hat, cut from black construction paper, a circle 3 inches in diameter. Now cut a circle 1 1/2 inches in diameter from the middle of the 3-inch circle. Save this little one for later. Cut a strip 5 x 2 1/2 inches. Cut little slits to form tabs along one long edge. Fold these tabs up. Now roll up this strip so it fits into the hole of the larger circle. Glue the tabs to the circle (brim of the hat). Take the small circle saved from above and glue it to the top of the hat.

These cute pilgrims can be used as table favors for Thanksgiving Dinner or as tray favors for a nursing home.

CORNHUSK TURKEY

by Linda Davidson

Here is a clever turkey made from cornhusks which you can find in the Mexican food section of your grocery store or perhaps in a craft store. You may use the cornhusks in their natural color or you may choose to tint them with food coloring.

Cut the body and head piece from brown construction paper. From red paper, cut a wattle, and from yellow or orange paper, cut a triangle for the nose.

Glue the cornhusks around the body to form tail feathers. Glue on the wattle and the nose. With black marker add lines for the neck, feet and eyes. And there you have a simple turkey for a Thanksgiving craft.

SOAP BOTTLE PILGRIMS

by Linda S. Davidson

You will need: detergent bottle for each figure, newspapers cut into strips, glue mixed with water, styrofoam balls (for head), scraps of fabric, yarn, beads, etc., paints.

Here is an easy way to make Pilgrims and Indians this Thanksgiving season. Cut out the V-section from the lower part of a soap bottle to form two legs (be careful cutting!). With papier-mache

strips, cover the head which is made with a styrofoam ball or wadded paper. Then cover the entire body (bottle) with the strips. Form arms with rolled paper. Join them to the body with more papier-mache. After adding several layers, let it dry completely. Then paint the figures. Add outfits made from scraps of material.

PINECONE TURKEY

You will need: real feathers or some made from construction paper, scissors, glue, crayons, pinecones.

Put the pinecone on its side. If you do not have real feathers available (like those used to make feather flowers) have children cut feathers from assorted colors of construction paper. Draw on vein designs. Glue feathers into top petals of the pinecone. Cut a head and neck piece from construction paper. (See illustration). Draw on an eye. Cut a red circle and glue it under the eye for a wattle. Glue the head to the bottom of the pinecone.

MAYFLOWER

You will need: clay, walnut shell halves, scissors, construction paper, glue, toothpicks.

Put a little piece of clay in the bottom of the walnut shell to hold the toothpicks. Cut 3 squares from construction paper. Make one smaller than the other two. Draw a design on the smaller one, if desired. Push toothpicks through tops and bottoms of squares. Leave enough toothpick at the bottom to push into the clay.

These can be used for table favors for Thanksgiving or they will float in the bathtub or a basin of water!

PICTURE YOUR THANKS

Create a collage of pictures of things for which you are thankful. Have available lots of old magazines and newspapers to cut up. Remember to think of not only material things, but look for blue skies (clean air), people (family and friends) and God (love).

Children may make individual collages on construction paper or the whole class can work on a big one on a bulletin board. Have them look through magazines and newspapers for appropriate pictures. Arrange

them as desired. Glue pictures onto construction paper or pin pictures to bulletin board. Title the bulletin board, "We Give Thanks to Thee, O Lord."

Send home the individual collages and encourage the children to display it on a refrigerator door or in their room where it will be highly visible. We cannot begin too early to make children aware of how many blessings they have.

PILGRIM DOLLS

Materials needed: white cotton fabric, permanent colored markers or crayons, glue, scissors, stuffing.

Have your class create Pilgrim dolls which require no sewing. Have each child draw a front and back for a doll, using exactly the same shape for both. Cut out the shapes. Cover work tables with a protective covering now. Next color the front and backs with markers, heavy crayons, or fabric paint. Be sure to work on only one piece at a time as the color may soak through. Then use a line of white glue around the edges and press the two pieces together. Leave an opening in which to insert the stuffing. Stuff and then glue the opening closed.

Or instead of everyone makin Pilgrm.

Or, instead of everyone making Pilgrims, have some children make Indians and then have the class re-enact the first Thanksgiving with their Indian and Pilgrim dolls.

APPLES

There is nothing like the taste of a fresh, crisp apple in the fall. Ask your class if they know about the legend of Johnny Appleseed. He planted apple orchards across many states. Also he was a very religious man, preaching about the love of mankind and nature as he roamed from town to town.

Try this apple turkey for Thanksgiving. Ask each child to bring an apple on Thanksgiving Sunday. In addition you will need: toothpicks, cranberries, raisins, large marshmallows.

The apple is the body of the turkey. Give each child 7 toothpicks for tail feathers. He/she should put cranberries on 4 of them and raisins on 3. A variation would be to use miniature marshmallows or strips of orange peel for feathers. Stick the 7 "feathers" into one end of the apple. For the neck place 3 raisins on one toothpick. Take one large marshmallow and cut out a "V" to make a beak and mouth. See the illustration. Push this on top of the neck toothpick. Two raisins can be added for eyes. Now push this into the other end of the apple, and you have your turkey.

THANK YOU, LORD, FOR...

by Jane K. Priewe

One month before Thanksgiving begin to talk about the many blessings we all enjoy. God gives us these gifts and we should thank Him daily for His generosity. On the Sunday you begin your project of pre-Thanksgiving preparation, suggest that the youngsters begin to go through newspapers, magazines, family snapshots, etc., hunting for pictures of things for which they are most grateful.

Cover a section of wall with plain white or autumn colored paper, or use a covered bulletin board. Print across the top, THANK YOU, LORD, FOR... Every Sunday encourage youngsters to bring pictures of things for which they are grateful. Tape or thumb tack the pictures to the wall or bulletin board. At first the display area will be sparsely covered, but in a few weeks, there will be pictures overlapping pictures.

You may get duplications of the same subjects, for more than one person can be thankful for the same thing. Seeing pictures about the same subject can only stress its importance.

On the last Sunday before Thanksgiving, you might like to clear the wall or bulletin board, and make a tally of the different pictures. The children will be interested to hear which subject was the most popular, and which were the most unusual. File the pictures because many of them will be helpful visual aids for future lessons. How great not to have to go any farther than your picture file to find just the right picture to make a particular point.

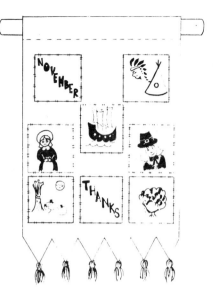

BANNER

by Linda S. Davidson

Here is a class project that each child will have a part in and the result will be a product of which they will be proud.

Decide first how many story squares you want. Then divide the class up, depending on its size, so that the youngsters work alone or in pairs or whatever on each square. Assign the subject for each square or let the children make up their own.

Use construction paper for the subjects to be drawn on. When pictures are complete, glue the paper onto felt pieces. Then button-hole stitch the felt onto a large piece of felt or burlap. Make a hem at the top and slip a wooden dowel through it to hang it by. Or tack it securely on a bulletin board. Share your banner with the whole congregation, and watch your class members proudly show it off!

THANKSGIVING DEVOTIONAL BOOKS

by Jane Landreth

Devotions can express thanks to God for His good gifts. During the Thanksgiving season, compile a booklet of daily devotions.

Using white sheets, fold them and place them in between a sheet of folded construction paper. On the front print, "My Thanksgiving Devotional Book." Decorate the front with illustrations of things for which you are thankful. Staple the folded edge of the construction paper and white paper to keep the pages connected.

Guide the children to explore ways to thank God for His good gifts. Let each child contribute to the booklet by duplicating each child's work for the others. The children can contribute poems, riddles, prayers, stories, and drawings to make the booklet of devotions.

Some good Bible verses to use are: Psalm 107:1, Psalm 103:2, James 1:17, Psalm 126:3, Psalm 145:21. The children can help to find other verses that tell of God's good gifts and care for them.

Let each child write his own introductory page. Guide each child to use the booklet to begin daily devotions at home.

O GIVE THANKS

by Jane Priewe

Here is a Thanksgiving activity which begins the first Sunday of November. It can be done by only one class, or be a competitive activity between classes of the same department or between departments. Regardless of how you decide to use the activity, by the Sunday before Thanksgiving, you should have an eye-catching poster which each child has helped to make.

On a large piece of colorful, poster paper draw a turkey's head on a fat body. Do not draw a full spread tail, because this will be the children's contribution. On the Sunday you mount your "un-tailed" turkey on the bulletin board or wall, tell the youngsters the tail will be formed by tracing around their hands on brown, grocery bag paper or autumn-colored construction paper. Cut out the hand and find a Bible verse from the Old or New Testament which deals with being thankful. Some form of the word thanks must be in the verse. "O give thanks unto the Lord; for he is good..." I Chronicles 16:34 or "Let us come before his presence with thanksgiving..." Psalm 95:2. Print or write the Bible verse on the palm of the cut-out hand, and bring the hand to church school next Sunday. Children can bring as many hands as they want, provided each hand has a different Bible verse on it.

As the cut-out hands are brought in, tape or thumb tack them (fingers away from the turkey) around the turkey's body. Let the hands overlap, and allow the fingers to hang free. This gives a lacy, three-dimensional effect to the tail as it grows from the addition of more and more hands each Sunday. You might like to let the youngsters share the Bible verses they find by reading them aloud before placing the cut-out hand on the turkey.

THANKSGIVING FILL IN

by Jane Landreth

There are many names in the Bible. Some of the names may be your name. Try to find as many of the names that fill in the Thanksgiving puzzle. If you need help use the reference verse.

T _ _ _ _ _ _
    2 Timothy 1:2
H _ _ _ _ _
    1 Samuel 2:1
A _ _ _
    Genesis 3:20
N _ _ _ _ _ _ _ _
    John 1:45
K _ _ _ _
    1 Chronicles 6:44
S _ _ _ _ _ _
    Acts 6:5
G _ _ _ _ _ _
    1 Samuel 17:4
I _ _ _ _ _
    Isaiah 1:1
V _ _ _ _ _
    Esther 1:9
I _ _ _ _
    Genesis 21:3
N _ _ _
    Genesis 6:8
G _ _ _ _ _
    Judges 6:11

Answers: Timothy, Hannah, Adam, Nathaniel, Kishi, Stephen, Goliath, Isaiah, Vashti, Isaac, Noah, Gideon

LET US GIVE THANKS

At this time of year Thanksgiving is an obvious theme for a bulletin board. Cover your bulletin board with yellow or orange paper or burlap. Make a large cornucopia out of dark brown paper. Have your class make fruits and vegetables from colored construction paper. Hand out sheets at least 6 x 12 inches so the fruits and vegetables will be large enough to be seen, and ask each child to make the food as large as that piece of paper. Place the fruits and vegetables in the mouth of the cornucopia. Make the letters from dark brown paper.

INDIAN SKINS

Materials needed: brown paper bags, paint or crayons or markers, scissors.

Go to the library and find some books which show Indian signs and their meanings. Display these books in your church school room and let the children study them. Then let them try making these Indian skins.

Open bags at the seams and flatten them. Cut out shapes to resemble animal hides. Wad them up in a ball to crumple the bags. Smooth out the bags and paint on Indian designs.

Have the class try to tell the Thanksgiving story using Indian symbols.

MAYFLOWER IN A BOTTLE

by Linda S. Davidson

You will need: Blue construction paper, crayons, scissors, clear plastic wrap, tape.

Here is a cute idea which is simple to make and most eye-catching. Have the children outline a bottle shape with a pencil (or trace a pattern which you provide) and then cut it out. Then have them turn the bottle shape on its side and draw a sailing ship to represent the Mayflower. (It would be helpful if you have a picture of the Mayflower or something similar for the children to see.) When they have completed their Mayflowers, give each one a piece of Saran Wrap or something similar. Roughly have them cut it in the bottle shape also; however, leave an inch or two extra margin all the way around it. Cover the front completely with the clear plastic wrap and tape the extra on the back. And there is a Mayflower in a bottle!

A HARVEST CRAFT

by Jean Rasmussen

Thanksgiving is harvest time, and the best harvest is God's fruits of the Spirit. The first three from Galatians 5:22 are: love, joy, peace.

That verse can be used on a fall wreath to increase our feeling of thankfulness to our Father.

MATERIALS:

White poster board 8" x 8", gold wool yarn 36", yellow felt 3" x 7", gold felt 3" x 7", light orange felt 3" x 6", dark orange felt 2" x 3", 3" x 5" index card, 2b pencil, ruler, black marker, punch, scissors, glue.

PROCEDURE:

Cut out all the patterns and trace them on the reverse side, so pencil marks won't show. Use the 2b pencil to trace the circle pattern on white poster board and cut it out.

Trace the large flower pattern nine times on the yellow felt and nine times on the gold felt. Cut out the flowers.

Trace the smaller flower pattern nine times on the light orange felt and cut out the flowers.

Trace the bud pattern nine times on the dark orange felt. Cut out the buds.

Punch a hole at the top of the wreath and then insert the 18" gold wool. Knot the gold wool and punch centers in the flower.

Arrange the flowers on the wreath and cut the remaining gold wool in three strips for the small bows. Place them on the wreath too and glue all pieces.

Print or type the verse, "The fruit of the Spirit is love, joy, peace..." Galatians 5:22 on the 3" x 5" index card. Outline it with the ruler and black marker. Cut it out and glue it to the lower part of the wreath.

Hang your wreath in a window and rejoice this Thanksgiving for the fruits given by God's Spirit.

"THE FRUIT OF THE SPIRIT IS LOVE, JOY, PEACE . . ." GALATIANS 5:22

THANKSGIVING MAGNET ART

by Jean Rasmussen

Thanksgiving is more than just a celebration of harvest time in thankfulness to the Father. It is also a time to launch out for God.

The Indians were fishermen, so a canoe of brown felt, with a magnet attached, can be a good Thanksgiving art project to be shared on the refrigerator.

MATERIALS: tan felt 3 1/2" x 7 1/2", brown yarn 24", thin cardboard 3 1/2" x 7 1/2", glue, pencil, black marker, ruler, 3" x 5" index card, scissors, small punch, 1 " magnet strip

PROCEDURE: Cut out and trace the canoe pattern on the light cardboard. Cut out the cardboard backing and punch out the holes on both sides. Trace the canoe pattern on the reverse side of the felt, so the pencil marks won't show. Glue the felt to the cardboard and punch out the holes for the yarn.

Cut a 24" piece of yarn in half and lace up the canoe sides. Use Scotch tape to secure the yarn on the back of the canoe at the top and bottom.

Using the 3" x 5" index card, print or type on the card, "Abounding with thanksgiving," Colossians 2:7. Outline it with the ruler and marker. Cut it out and glue it to the right front of the canoe.

Attach the magnet strip to the center cardboard backing.

Indians caught fish, not only to eat, but to bury with kernels of corn for a rich harvest. This canoe magnet art can enrich the lives of others by reminding them to abound with thanksgiving toward the Father.

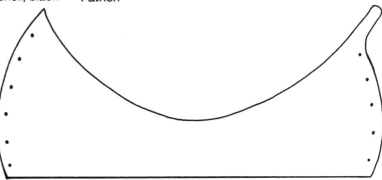

(Enlarge illustration to 7 1/2")

THANKFULNESS SYMBOLS

by Phyllis Vos Wezeman

In this activity participants are asked to cut or draw a symbol of something for which they are especially thankful. These shapes may be used as nametags. An additional idea to use at the conclusion of the class or session is to combine the symbols into a thankfulness collage which could be displayed in the room or on a bulletin board in the church hallway.

Materials:
- Construction paper
- Scissors
- Markers
- Pins
- Posterboard, optional
- Glue, optional

Method: Before the session or class begins, cut the construction paper into quarter-size pieces.

As participants arrive have them choose a piece of paper to serve as their nametag. Invite them to cut a shape out of the paper, or to draw a symbol on it, which will convey something for which they are thankful. For example, the shape of a person could represent a family member or special friend, a Bible may stand for God's love and a flower could signify the beauty of Creation.

When the symbols are completed, ask each person to write his or her name on them. Provide pins and ask participants to wear them as nametags. Take turns going around the entire group sharing names and a few sentences about the meaning of the symbols.

If desired, at the conclusion of the session combine the shapes into a Thanksgiving Collage by glueing them to a piece of posterboard. Display it in the classroom or church.

SPOONIE STORIES

by Phyllis Vos Wezeman

Recycled disposable plastic spoons, or inexpensive wooden cooking spoons, can become quick and easy puppets. Since food, especially the traditional turkey dinner, is a focal point of Thanksgiving Day, spoon puppets are an effective tool to use in telling the tale of the first holiday in Plymouth, Massachussetts.

Materials:
- Spoons
- Permanent markers
- Tacky glue
- Yarn, or material for hair
- Fabric scraps
- Scissors
- Pipe cleaner, optional

Method: Create a variety of Pilgrim and Indian puppets. Tan colored plastic spoons could be used to make the Indians, or color may be added to white ones with marker. Using permanent marker, draw a face on the curved, bottom side of the spoon.

Make hair by winding several strands of yarn around a few fingers, tying it in the center and cutting open the loops. Glue it to the top of the head. Cotton or felt may be used instead.

Make a simple costume by cutting a rectangle or triangle of fabric the length of the distance from the neck to the bottom of the spoon. Cut a small slit one-quarter inch from the top of the costume and slide the spoon through it. Glue the costume in place on both sides of the neck. If more elaborate clothing is desired, additional fabric may be layered or added. Trims, such as feathers for the Indians, may be attached. Make capes and hats for the Pilgrims.

If desired, arms may be made of felt or a pipe cleaner and attached to the body.

Read a book about the first Thanksgiving and act out the story with the puppets.

GRATITUDE GALLERY

by Phyllis Vos Wezeman

This community building activity not only encourages participants to get acquainted with one another but also provides them with an opportunity to express gratitude to God for the many gifts they have been given. It could be used effectively at an intergenerational event such as a church supper.

Materials:
- White paper, 8 1/2" x 11"
- Markers
- Masking tape

Method: Distribute a sheet of paper and a marker to each participant. Instruct the group to fold the paper in quarters and then re-open it. Ask each person to write or draw the following information in each quarter of the paper:

Upper Left: Name, town and one thing about their family

Upper Right: One or several things for which they are thankful

Lower Left: A special talent, skill, ability or interest for which they are thankful

Lower Right: A way in which they will express gratitude to God for His special gifts

When the sheets are completed, have each person get a piece of masking tape and use it to attach the paper to the wall. When all participants have posted a sheet invite the group to walk through the "art gallery" to learn about each other. Encourage everyone to browse, read and take notes on any people in particular they want to talk with during or after the session. After a short time, invite each person to stand by his or her sheet on the wall. Take turns having people introduce themselves by name and tell one thing for which they are especially thankful. Ask the group to affirm each other by clapping for the multiple gifts and talents that are shared by these people. Participants should return to their seats. Conclude the activity with a brief time of silent reflection on God's goodness which has been evidenced in so many ways.

RESOURCES

The Thanksgiving Story by Alice Dalgliesh, Scribners, 1954.

Turkeys, Pilgrims, and Indian Corn by Edna Barth, Clarion Books, 1975.

Pilgrim Children on the Mayflower by Ida DeLage, Garrard, 1981.

If You Sailed the Mayflower by Ann McGovern, Scholastic Book Services, 1975.

Margaret Pumphrey's Pilgrim Stories revised by Elvajean Hall. Illustrated by Jon Nielsen. Chicago: Rand McNally & Company, 1961.

Thanksgiving Feast and Festival compiled by Mildred Correll Luckhardt. Illustrated by Ralph McDonald. Nashville: Abingdon Press, 1966.

It's Time for Thanksgiving by Elizabeth Hough Sechrist and Janette Woolsey. Illustrated by Guy Fry. Philadelphia: Macrae Smith Company, 1957.

The Plymouth Thanksgiving by Leonard Weisgard. Garden City, NY: Doubleday & Co., 1967.

The Coming of the Pilgrims by E. Brooks Smith and Robert Meredith. Boston: Little, Brown and Co., 1964.

ABOUT THE AUTHORS

JANICE BACON is the former Director of Christian Education at the Hingham Congregational Church in Hingham, Massachussetts.

LINDA DAVIDSON is a former church school teacher and V.P. at Educational Ministries, Inc. She and husband Robert reside in Diamond Bar, CA.

ROBERT DAVIDSON is president of Educational Ministries, Inc., editor of Church Educator, and the author of several books on youth programming.

NEIL FITZGERALD is a retired English teacher from South Dartmouth, presently involved in free-lance writing and the Junior Great Books Program. His stories, poetry, plays, and articles have appeared in over one hundred publications nationwide.

JANE LANDRETH is a Christian educator and free-lance writer from Republic, MO. She has had over 525 articles and stories published in various religious magazines. She also teaches in religious education conferences and holds seminars in many states.

JANE PRIEWE is a free-lance writer whose articles have appeared in many national publications. She has sold 1,300 stories or articles. She resides in Alhambra, California.

JEAN RASMUSSEN is a free-lance writer and a member of The Presbyterian Church at Woodbury. She lives in Wenonah, New Jersey.

JUDY GATTIS SMITH is the author of several books and has been active in Christian education for many years. She leads workshops and delivers keynote speeches on Christian education throughout the country. She is married to a United Methodist minister and lives in Lynchburg, Virginia.

ELAINE WARD is the author of several books, leads Christian education workshops across the country, and writes for various religious publications. She now lives in Lancaster, PA.

ROBERT WARD is a free-lance writer from Newman, Georgia.

PHYLLIS VOS WEZEMAN is the Director of the Religious Arts and Education Ministry for the United Religious Community in South Bend, Indiana.

EVELYN WITTER is a free-lance writer from Milan, Illinois. She writes for many religious education publications. She has taught church school for 15 years.

CREATIVE IDEAS FOR ADVENT

edited by Robert G. Davidson

Every church should have one or more copies of this book from which the staff and lay leaders can gather ideas to implement during the holiday season. A wealth of suggestions for special programs, displays, family activities, and more have been collected in this resource.

This creative planning aid is conveniently divided into three sections—All Church Activities, Children's Activities, and Youth Activities. None of the material, however, has to be limited to only one area of programming. Material can be drawn together from any of the three sections to best benefit your needs.

Item: 2516 $12.95
ISBN 0-940754-06-1

CREATIVE IDEAS FOR ADVENT, Volume 2

edited by Robert and Linda Davidson

If you have used **Creative Ideas for Advent,** you will be excited to learn of its sequel, **Volume 2**. This is another valuable resource that every church staff should have to participate fully in the joy and celebration of the Advent season.

This creative planning aid is conveniently divided into four major sections—All Church Activities, Children's Activities, Youth Activities, and Family Activities. In its pages you will find Advent wreath services, children's Christmas stories, activity projects, service projects, meditations, lesson plans, puzzles, games, plays, and a host of other resource articles that will provide a new approach to traditional Christmas festivities.

Item: 2526 $12.95
ISBN 0-940754-35-5

CREATIVE IDEAS FOR LENT

edited by Robert G. Davidson

After the successful response to **Creative Ideas for Advent,** we now offer a similar fine resource for Lent. In its more than one hundred pages, this book includes intergenerational events, worship ideas, activity projects, youth programs, lesson plans, stories, and many other ideas for use during the Lenten season.

The material is divided into three major sections—All Church Activities, Children's Activities, and Youth Activities. This does not mean that any of the material has to be limited to certain age groups. The possibilities are infinite of how you can use the ideas in this book.

Item: 2521 $12.95
ISBN 0-940754-25-8

CREATIVE IDEAS FOR LENT, Volume 2

edited by Robert and Linda Davidson

Due to the popularity of **Creative Ideas for Lent,** we have edited another seasonal resource. Here you will find more materials to make your Lenten programs truly memorable. Included in this volume you will find several plays, worship services, intergenerational events, crafts for children, study program ideas, meditations, puzzles and quizzes, youth programs, and much more.

In addition to the three regular sections—All Church Activities, Children's Activities, and Youth Activities—we have added a new one, Family Activities. We hope people will find material here to use both at church and in individual homes to make the Easter event more meaningful to each member of the family.

Item: 2531 $12.95
ISBN 0-940754-62-2

Order from:

EDUCATIONAL MINISTRIES, INC.

Call toll free: 800-221-0910